Religious Dimensions in Literature

Lee A. Belford, Editor

Religious Dimensions in Literature

THE SEABURY PRESS · NEW YORK

1982
The Seabury Press
815 Second Avenue
New York, N.Y. 10017

Printed in the United States of America

Library of Congress Cataloging in Publication Data

Main entry under title:
Religious dimensions in literature.
        Contents: Charles Williams' All Hallows' Eve / introduction and com-
    mentary by Edmund Fuller—C.S. Lewis' Till we have faces / introduc-
    tion and commentary by Nathan Comfort Starr—Albert Camus'
    The plague / introduction and commentary by Thomas Merton—[etc.]
        1. Religion in literature—Addresses, essays, lectures
2. Literature, Modern—20th century—History and criticism
—Addresses, essays, lectures.   I. Belford, Lee Archer, 1913—
PN49.I68   809'.93382   81-14390
ISBN 0-8164-2360-1   AACR2

Grateful acknowledgment is made to the following publishers for permission to
use, under the fair-use provision, copyrighted material from the titles listed:

Farrar, Straus & Giroux (The Noonday Press): Charles Williams, *All Hallows' Eve*.
    Copyright © by Pellegrini and Cudahy.
Geoffrey Bles: *Letters of C.S. Lewis*, ed. W.H. Lewis; C.S. Lewis, *Till We Have
    Faces;* and *Light on C.S. Lewis*, ed. Jocelyn Gibb.
Harcourt Brace Jovanovich: C.S. Lewis, *Of Other Worlds* and *The Four Loves*.
Oxford University Press: C.S. Lewis, *The Allegory of Love* and Charles Williams,
    Arthurian Torso.
The Macmillan Company: C.S. Lewis, *The Great Divorce* and *The Weight of Glory*.
Alfred A. Knopf, Inc.: Albert Camus, *Notebooks* and *The Plague*.
Harcourt Brace Jovanovich: T.S. Eliot, *Collected Poems 1909-1962*, copyright
    © 1936 by Harcourt Brace and World; copyright © 1943, 1963, 1964 by T.S. Eliot.
Farrar, Straus & Giroux: Walker Percy, *The Last Gentleman*.

Contents

Preface

Human beings want to share their experiences with others—from the simplest physical adventure ("I think it's the coldest day I've ever known!") to the most profound brush with the world of the mind or the spirit. Even in an age when many thinkers have begun to fear that people have forgotten how to read, books still provide companionship and stimulation for many. And it is always frustrating for the dedicated reader to discover a fascinating book and have no one to talk to about it. Building on this understanding, churches have for many years sought to draw adult Christians into grappling with the meaning and problems of the world and the spirit through book discussion groups. An adult leader, or a steering committee of group members, will choose a list of provocative books in advance and assign a session or sessions to discussions of each.

In the 1960's The Seabury Press first published a group of unusually thoughtful and perceptive discussion guides to a group of outstanding literary works addressing the human condition—both moral and spiritual. The commentators who prepared the discussions were themselves prominent thinkers, writers, and educators. Their essays and suggestions for discussion point the way for a group coming to grips with a serious literary work. These commentaries do not pose all the questions that could be asked, but they open the door to what could be a vitally important sharing for the participants.

Adult book discussion groups have remained popular in many church settings and the books and commentators chosen more than a decade ago remain pertinent and alive today. It was decided, therefore, to collect the most interesting of the commentaries (which were originally issued in booklet form) in one volume and make them available to another generation of questors.

The books presented in this volume do not, by any stretch of the imagination, present a single point of view or a unified world vision. The only connecting thread is that each author represented was, through his work, attempting to come to grips with the spiritual dimension of life—with the *beyond*. Charles Williams, for instance, was a Christian who apparently never had a major crisis in regard to his belief—his view of the world of the living and the world of the dead was grounded in a solid faith. In contrast, C.S. Lewis, who was at one point in his life a nominal and diffident Christian, had experienced what is likened to a conversion experience in his mature years which altered completely his way of looking at things. Something similar evidently happened to T.S. Eliot, who was converted to Anglicanism and became an ardent supporter of the Anglo-Catholic tradition. Walker Percy, a Southern American, was converted to Roman Catholicism and has published many philosophical and theological essays as well as novels. His work has been much influenced by the writing of Søren Kierkegaard. Albert Camus was disdainful of Christianity—which does not mean that he was not religious. Thomas Merton suggests that Camus was repelled by the perversion of pure Christianity which he saw reflected in the beliefs and lives of the Christians he knew.

And just as the writers represented here have different points of view about the human condition and the relationship of humans to God, so their books represent different kinds of literature. Charles Williams' *All Hallows' Eve* is a visionary novel in which some of the leading characters are dead. Impossible things happen and yet there is logic and meaning to what ensues. Lewis' *Till We Have Faces* is based on the myth of Cupid and Psyche as told by Apuleius, and becomes its own myth in presenting the tyranny of possessive love and a journey towards redemption. *The Plague* of Albert Camus deals with a dramatic situation in a small town in North Africa in a completely realistic fashion, and yet one recognizes the plague that infects every society and befalls every man. Will Barrett, in Walker Percy's *The Last Gentleman,* is a young man on a pilgrimage in search of himself and his journey leads him from New York through the South and on to New Mexico. In discussing the work of poet T.S. Eliot, it is especially helpful to have a commentator, and a learned one, for Eliot used as his raw material the myths, legends, and beliefs of classical literature, East and West.

The writers of the commentaries were chosen because they were sensitive to the questions asked and the problems posed in the given book. In many cases, the commentators were friends of the authors and these friendships gave them deeper insights into the concerns that were being expressed. Each of the commentaries presents essential data about the author, summarizes the book briefly, shows its place in literature, and then discusses the themes and issues embodied in it, putting these themes and issues in a religious perspective.

The commentators in this book are a model for showing the sort of things that might be discussed. One may not and need not always agree with them, but their observations sharpen one's acuity and deepen one's insights. And no commentator could pose all of the questions one might ask about any one of these truly seminal and provocative works. But if they help open the doors to a sincere and lively discussion of religion and of the religious dimension of life, they have fulfilled their purpose. It is for the group, wherever it may be, to go beyond the doors into other worlds of understanding.

Lee A. Belford

All Hallows' Eve

An Introduction and Commentary

All Hallows' Eve is the last and most demanding of Charles Williams' seven remarkable novels, his supernatural thrillers. Finished not long before his death in 1945, it carries to their highest complexity of form the ideas and images which are present in his novels from first to last as a continuity, growth, or refinement.

About the Author

Who was Charles Williams? In proportion to the quality, volume, and slowly but steadily increasing reputation and appreciation of his work, he has been a surprisingly obscure figure. He was born on September 20, 1886, in what was then the suburbs of London, since swallowed up by the greater city. He came from a lower-middle-class background.

The Williamses were economically pinched, but it was a happy, loving home, and devoutly Christian. Charles grew from childhood within the Church, well educated in his faith, and he never experienced a falling away from his belief or a major crisis of doubt—unusual for one who penetrated so deeply beyond conventional religious expression and understood so well the crises of faith and the possibilities of evil.

In his boyhood the family moved to St. Albans, and Charles went, on a scholarship won by his own abilities, to St. Albans Grammar School. Later he had two years, again on scholarship, at University College, Gower Street, London. But the family's economic squeeze interrupted that, and his formal education was at an end. His real education was beginning. Williams was a natural scholar of depth, and he was to explore both knowledge and wisdom as long as he lived. In 1908 he joined Oxford University Press in the necessary and demanding—but tedious—capacity of proofreader. This occupation, scholarly in its patterns, became for him an important medium of learning. Later, during the years of World War II, in Oxford, the largely self-educated Williams made a place for himself, and won respect and love in a formidable circle of University scholars and writers whose peer he was in all respects.

At Amen House, near St. Paul's, in the heart of some of the terrain of *All Hallows' Eve*, Williams worked for eight years as a proofreader before his gradual rise in function, influence, and appreciation in the work of the Press. He always felt that he owed a great deal to the Press, to Sir Humphrey Milford, its Director, and others there. Certainly that is true. What I also believe is true, but with which I believe Williams sincerely would not have agreed, is that Oxford Press can be criticized for so long using so distinguished a man in such minor capacities.

In 1917, when he was thirty, he married Florence Conway, with whom he had been in love for years, out of which experience had come some of his early poetry, especially the sonnet sequence called *The Silver Stair* (1912), not his first writing, but his first published book. One son was born of this marriage: Michael. It was a good marriage, important in the shaping of the man. His wife and son survived him.

The years of World War I, including the early years of his marriage, were a time of inward crisis and suffering, his deepest encounter up till then with the awareness of evil, darkness, and destruction loose in the world; the realization, as expressed in *All Hallows' Eve*, that "the universe is always capable of a worse trick than we suppose. . . ." His profoundly grounded faith, his foundation of parental love, the new sustaining of married love all combined to keep him firm so that suffering transformed itself into knowledge and growth, leading to the codicil to the above statement: "but at least when we have known it we are no longer surprised by anything less."

His literary output was large and diverse, including the novels, a great deal of poetry (the principal achievement in which is the Arthurian poems *Taliessin Through Logres* and *The Region of the Summer Stars*), plays, biographies, critical studies, and theological writings. *The Figure of Beatrice* is a major contribution to Dante studies. *The Descent of the Dove,* one of his best-kno·vn books, is a history of the work of the Holy Spirit in the Church, a splendid interpretation of Church history.

In World War II, as the bombing of London was intensified, Oxford Press moved its operations from Amen House (which soon after was totally destroyed) to its parent city of Oxford. Quite a few years before that, Williams and C. S. Lewis had come to know each other by the exchange of letters of mutual admiration, respectively for *The Place of the Lion* and *The Allegory of Love.* Their acquaintance had widened to include a number of Lewis's Oxford friends.

Upon Williams' removal to Oxford there followed several years of intensive association among this band of brothers (and occasionally a sister: Dorothy L. Sayers). The masculine company, in particular, met almost every Tuesday morning at a pub and almost every Thursday evening in Lewis's rooms at Magdalen College. In the evening sessions, there was a regular reading aloud, with criticism, of work in progress. All of Lewis's *Perelandra,* Williams' *All Hallows' Eve,* and a large part of J. R. R. Tolkien's *Lord of the Rings* trilogy were read aloud at those sessions. There was an immense cross fertilization of creative ideas and sharpening of skills among these men and the others.

Williams, meanwhile, was enjoying the fullest recognition of his high abilities. He created an intellectual ferment as a lecturer and tutor at Oxford, where he received an honorary M.A. This was the full life that came to a shockingly abrupt, unforeshadowed end on May 15, 1945. He had entered Radcliffe Infirmary as the result of a sudden onset of pain a few days before, and had undergone an emergency operation, after which he never regained full consciousness. His friends, in Oxford and London, were stunned.

C. S. Lewis wrote a superb and loving sketch of the man, describing his nature and abilities, his bond with the Oxford circle, and the sudden shock of his death. It is the Preface to *Essays Presented to Charles Williams* (Oxford University Press). This is a collection of six essays by members of the group: Dorothy L. Sayers, J. R. R. Tolkien, C. S. Lewis, W. H. Lewis, A. Owen Barfield, and Gervase Mathew. They had assembled these papers, planning to present them to Williams as a tribute of admiration and affection to mark his expected removal from Oxford back to London at the close of the war. Instead, it became a memorial volume. It has been out of print for some time, but is available in libraries and can occasionally be had secondhand.

The indispensable full-length biographical-critical study of Williams is *An Introduction to Charles Williams,* by Alice Mary Hadfield (London: Robert Hale, 1959). The title is too modest. Because of its comprehensiveness, and the circumstance that Mrs. Hadfield was for a number of years his colleague at Oxford Press and a close friend, it is not likely to be superseded for some time to come. *The Theology of Romantic Love; A Study in the Writings of Charles Williams,* by Mary McDermott Shideler (New York: Harper & Row, 1962), is important for any comprehensive study of Williams, but it is unfortunately heavy-handed and turgid and thus unrewarding to the general reader.

I have discussed the rest of the novels and other aspects of Williams' work, together with that of Lewis and Tolkien, in *Books with Men Behind Them* (New York: Random House, 1962).

Mrs. Hadfield believes (as does Lewis) that all the rest of Williams' total aggregate of friends meant as much to him, and received as much from him, as that particular band of Oxford literary friends. The themes and stories of some of Williams' writings, and the word-of-mouth dissemination by which groups of enthusiasts are apt to discover him together, hold the dangers of possible cult formation. Mrs. Hadfield observes of "C. W.," as most of his friends called him, that "those with a sense of need were ready to adore him. But his 'See thou do it not' and his laughter always prevented it. He never mistook himself for the work, nor doubted that he himself must work as hard as those he helped on the way. No cult could survive an hour's conversation and laughter with C. W." This should be remembered by those admirers who did not know the man.

All the same, his personal qualities, like the work, were unusual and memorable. To his friends, she says, in words once applied to Kierkegaard, he was "God's spy in his generation."

C. S. Lewis said, "No event has so corroborated my faith in the next world as Williams did simply by dying. When the idea of death and the idea of Williams thus met in my mind, it was the idea of death that was changed."

Introduction to the Book

Before we attempt an interpretation of *All Hallows' Eve*, there follows, as an aid to memory or to reading, a chapter by chapter synopsis of the story. It is merely the skeleton of the plot, the frame, the "melodrama." The true drama, the meaning, the ultimate story, lies deeper. In the discussion there will be recapitulations of parts of this synopsis, reviewed in examining their larger significance.

CHAPTER 1

JUST at the close of the European phase of World War II, a young woman named Lester Furnival stands on Westminster Bridge, London—dead. She had been killed, a moment before, by the accidental crash of a military plane which fell close to her. She sees her husband, Richard, approaching (they had been married six months), and when he draws near, asks him, with a gesture like a rejection, why he is late. He appears pale and startled, asks her why she is there and what she means, then seems to recede or fade away. It is only then that she realizes she is dead.

She begins to walk. The streets are familiar but strangely empty, as if the buildings were mere façades. She encounters a friend, Evelyn Mercer, and remembers that they had planned to meet. Evelyn is dead, too; killed simultaneously. Nervous and frightened, Evelyn clings to Lester.

They wander through their familiar yet strange environment. Lester ponders her situation. Evelyn babbles, weeps, and whines; she is essentially a complainer, a hater, a gossip. Lester is evaluating her own marriage, shaken by the encounter with Richard, conscious of loving him, but also aware of shortcomings in their brief married life. To Evelyn she says, "Let's do something now." But neither of them knows what to do.

CHAPTER 2

ABOUT a month after the accident, Richard Furnival calls on his friend Jonathan Drayton, a painter. Jonathan speaks of being "practically engaged" to Betty Wallingford, but says that her mother, Lady Wallingford, is not pleased about it.

He shows Richard two recent paintings. One is a scene of London after a raid, characterized by an exceptional quality of light which suggests "Creation" to Richard. Jonathan says he doesn't quite know how he captured it. The other is a portrait, not from life, of a man called Simon the Clerk, a religious cultist who has caused a great stir in the West. There are similar men in Russia and China, and opinion is arising that these three "spiritual leaders" should meet in the possible hope of resolving the problems of the world, political and spiritual alike.

In the imaginative painting, the Clerk is a huge beetle-shaped figure with a curiously empty face. His throng of followers appear to be a horde of small beetles, streaming toward a cleft of rock. Lady Wallingford arrives with Betty. She is shown the portrait, which she had suggested Jonathan should paint. It angers her and she accuses him of painting "our Father" as an "imbecile." The scene is tense. Richard perceives that Betty is frightened and upset. The women depart.

Richard thinks of going to see Simon the Clerk for himself. He wishes Lester were alive, for she had known Betty, and he thinks she might have been helpful. As he goes out into the city, thinking of his dead wife, he sees her, across a street, as he has seen her a number of times, but she is gone, then, with no direct encounter.

CHAPTER 3

SIMON the Clerk unexpectedly calls at Jonathan's studio to see the painting. Unlike Lady Wallingford, he admires it, fascinated by the intuitive truth to which Jonathan had penetrated. Viewing the painting of the city, he dismisses it as false, saying that if Jonathan would follow him for a year he would see it as he does. Though puzzled, Jonathan is glad that the Clerk is not angry and hopes he may help his cause with Betty, about whom he feels disquieting premonitions of some kind of danger.

As the Clerk leaves, we follow him and are told something of his nature and origins. Born in France of Jewish parents, he is a caba-list, a magician, nearly two hundred years old. We learn that Betty is, in fact, his daughter, conceived and nurtured for a purpose of his own, in which Lady Wallingford is his servant-accomplice.

CHAPTER 4

BETTY thinks of odd patterns in her life—in London, where she is a young lady, and at a small house in Yorkshire, where Lady Wallingford takes her from time to time and treats her as a servant, in a kind of "training." She has also been told that she is adopted. At school she had known Lester and Evelyn, liking Lester but disliking Evelyn, who behaved maliciously toward her.

While Betty thinks of these things, Lady Wallingford summons her to the Clerk. She is to be sent into the city on a strange errand which she has performed before, the nature of which she does not understand. What happens, unknown to her, is that the Clerk magically separates her soul from her body, and sends her spirit into the city while her flesh remains behind. The city in which Betty's detached spirit walks is the same as that in which the dead Lester and Evelyn move. In this place, all time exists simultaneously. Her unrealized errand (of which, "being magically commanded," she is therefore both ignorant and innocent) is to read newspapers of future dates and bring back information about the future to the Clerk, of which she remembers nothing when reunited with her body.

At the same time, Lester and Evelyn are wandering the city, Lester still searching for the meaning of past and present, Evelyn still fretting. The girls catch a glimpse of Betty. Evelyn calls to her, and they run after her. Betty, startled at seeing them, runs away, frightened of Evelyn. They follow Betty all the way to Lady Wallingford's house, into which she vanishes.

Lester had told Evelyn to leave Betty alone, as she had done in their girlhood. Outside this house, Lester suddenly senses an anguished need from Betty within. She is tempted to turn away, and Evelyn tries to draw her off, but with an abrupt realization of what she should do, though she does not know why, Lester enters the house.

CHAPTER 5

RICHARD goes to the Clerk's headquarters. It is a place where some of his followers, whom he has cured of diseases, now live, serving him. There is an air of peace and calm, all the talk is of "love" and "the Father." Richard feels its spell, but at the same time has an intuitive, backward-tugging sense that it is an "unhallowed peace." Simon receives him, inviting him to come to a ritual called "the Relaxation." The Clerk presides, speaking in a strange voice, variously in Hebrew and English, talking of "love" and mystical matters. The words seems to have hypnotic power as sounds rather than meaning. During this peculiar rite, through Lady Wallingford's thoughts, we learn more of the Clerk. She has served him and borne Betty to him, conceived not in love but in deliberate calculation. We learn, too, that the "spiritual leaders" in Russia and China, with whom he is urged to meet, are magical duplications, projections of himself. When the time comes to reunite them with himself, he will have gained all power over men, political and spiritual.

Richard, almost caught in the spell, remembers Lester and recovers himself. He is appalled to see a presence enter, as if through the wall, approach the Clerk and talk with him. It is Lester's friend, Evelyn. Richard realizes that he is in the presence of a powerful evil.

CHAPTER 6

LESTER enters Lady Wallingford's house (close of Chapter 4). Simon senses her presence but does not realize who or what she is. He and Lady Wallingford depart for his headquarters. Lester goes to Betty's room and waits beside the bed. Betty, weak and pale, opens her eyes, greets her, and then falls into sleep. Lester remains at her side until she awakens, markedly refreshed. They talk of their schoolgirl days. Lester speaks of times when she and Evelyn had not been kind to Betty. She asks her forgiveness, which Betty grants radiantly, deprecating the need for it. Betty expresses a dread of Evelyn, but Lester says she will deal with her. Betty speaks of a dream or vision she had as an infant—seeming to be submerged in water, to be lifted out of it on the back of a powerful fish, then taken up by a nurse who said, "No-one can undo that; bless God for it."

Evelyn, who had waited outside when Lester entered the house, wanders off alone. Feeling herself drawn, she goes to the Clerk's place, enters, and approaches him (Chapter 5). He greets her and she feels comfort, satisfaction, and abatement of fear. Willingly she clings to him.

Chapter 7

RICHARD goes from the Clerk's meeting to Jonathan, and they talk of the sinister events, Richard worrying lest Simon should attempt to control Lester as he appears to influence Evelyn. They look at the London painting Simon had hated. The light seems to have intensified, and they realize that somehow it represents another City than the ordinary one. They decide to go to Lady Wallingford's and see what is happening to Betty—and possibly to Lester, for Richard has a feeling she may be there.

The Clerk is about to fulfill the purpose for which he intends Betty to be used. He is going to kill her by magic spells and dispatch her soul under magical control to be his permanent servant in that other world.

Unknown to him, Lester is beside the bed as Simon begins his powerful incantations over Betty. She understands nothing except her friend's danger and need, for she sees that Betty is dying. Spontaneously she interposes herself between her friend and the spell. The struggle is prolonged and intense. Lester is almost engulfed by the deathly spell, but feels herself miraculously sustained, as by the framework of a cross, as she makes her willing substitution for the victim. The Clerk does not understand what has happened, but his operation fails.

Jonathan and Richard are announced, and thrust their way into the room before they can be refused. Betty greets them eagerly. Richard and Lester see each other, and she tells him she will wait for him. Temporarily defeated, Lady Wallingford and the Clerk withdraw.

Chapter 8

SENSING that Evelyn is involved, the Clerk questions her and learns enough to realize that it was Lester who frustrated his designs upon Betty. Wishing to use Evelyn to entrap Lester, he promises to "give" Betty to her if she will bring Lester to him. Evelyn consents, but feels a moment of intense agony as she passes under his control.

Evelyn goes to Lester and Betty and asks Lester to come with her. Puzzled, Lester consents, willing to help Evelyn also. When the girls go to the Clerk, Lester watches while he keeps another promise to Evelyn—to make a body for her. He creates a dwarfish, malformed woman's body. When it is done, Evelyn wishes to enter it and have it for herself alone, but Simon says both girls must share it. He believes it will entrap Lester, but she enters it willingly, though with a certain repugnance, feeling that she may be able to help Evelyn. This intention makes it useless as the intended trap. The dwarf body, doubly occupied, goes into the city.

CHAPTER 9

JONATHAN takes Betty to find her old nurse, hoping to clarify the vision of the water (Chapter 6). The good old woman tells of being distressed that the infant Betty was not baptized. Secretly, fearfully, she had taken water, prayed God to bless it, and baptized the child, unknown to Lady Wallingford. This was what had lodged in Betty's mind as a symbolic dream. Jonathan is determined that Betty shall not go back to Lady Wallingford or the Clerk. They telephone Richard to say they are coming to him.

The dwarf woman has been wandering the streets, talking to itself much of the time in Evelyn's voice. Taking control, Lester phones Richard and says that she is coming to see him, telling him of the strange hulk she occupies. Richard, Jonathan, and Betty are all there when the dwarf arrives. As Lester, through this instrument, is talking to them, Evelyn breaks in as if to claim Betty (promised her by the Clerk), saying, "I want to see Betty cry." Lester takes control again, and says she must return this "thing" they occupy to the Clerk. They depart in a cab, Lester and Betty trying to help Evelyn, who will not be helped.

CHAPTER 10

IT is All Hallows' Eve. The Clerk, in his hall, has prepared a small image of Betty, with one of her hairs in it. He plans to kill her magically by piercing it with a long steel needle. Lady Wallingford is holding the image in the ritual, when by accident she moves and is pricked by the needle. Her blood, flowing onto the image, makes her an unintended substitution for Betty, and she realizes that she is likely to die in place of her. Because of the blunder, and because his other spells had been deflected previously, the Clerk's operations begin to miscarry and to twist back upon him.

At this moment, Jonathan, Richard, Betty, and the dwarf arrive, Evelyn within it screaming to be let in to the Clerk's house. His followers are aroused, and as his powers fail, they are suddenly afflicted again with the diseases from which he had "cured" them. The dwarf rushes toward the Clerk, dragging Betty. Jonathan tries to restrain Betty from going into the circle of danger, but she rebuffs him, willing to substitute herself to save Evelyn. As Betty comes near, Simon tries to stab her throat with his long needle, but Lady Wallingford, who had been thrust aside, bleeding, with the magic image, clutches at him and deflects his thrust.

A mystical holy rain penetrates the building and dissolves the dwarf figure, diminishing the Clerk's collapsing powers. The beneficent presence of All Saints is overcoming him. His spells have curved inward. He sees his two projections of himself coming toward him, prematurely and unsummoned. The spells he invokes to stop them work equally against himself. They come together and he is mysteriously consumed.

Evelyn's soul flees from help to wander again. Lester takes a loving departure from Richard, to go permanently into the depths of the Holy City to await him there. Lady Wallingford is barely alive, but Betty assumes her care. Before leaving with Jonathan and Richard, Betty expends her spiritual energy in an act of merciful self-giving by which, through the grace of the City, the ignorant victims of the Clerk's false teaching and healing are truly healed.

Discussion of the Themes

The principal themes of *All Hallows' Eve* are, first: the simultaneous existence, the interpenetration, the coinherence of what we commonly (and erroneously as we shall see) call the "natural" and the "supernatural"; second: substituted love, in the Incarnational sense of the free offering to take upon oneself the sufferings of another; third: the essential holiness of all things except some consciously chosen attitudes of the will, from which the corrupt use of anything else proceeds. It is not that these themes and the subordinate ideas developed within them are so much overtly, insistently stated, but rather that they permeate the whole body of *story, enacted idea,* which is Williams' medium here.

An aspect of the book, perhaps not sharply enough defined to be classed as a theme, is that of Purgatory, insofar as there is a process or series of stages by which the soul, after the body's death, pre-pares itself (or fails to do so) at greater or lesser speed, for full realization of its new state of being and for entrance into the inner precincts of the City of God—another idea important to Williams. It is, in fact, a picture of the difficult process of growing into holi-ness or blessedness.

In reading this, and the rest of Williams' novels, or other such imaginative, theologically rooted stories, a warning must be kept in mind. C. S. Lewis put it into the mouth of the man he called his "Master," George MacDonald, who appears as a character in Lewis's *The Great Divorce*. That is Lewis's answer to Blake's *The Marriage of Heaven and Hell*. More intensely and specifically than *All Hallows' Eve*, it is a Purgatorial story, dealing wholly with the soul's choices and purifications after bodily death.

In *The Great Divorce*, George MacDonald serves Lewis as guide and teacher as Virgil served Dante through Hell and Purgatory. At the end he cautions him: "Ye can know nothing of the end of all things, or nothing expressible in those terms. . . . Do not ask of a vision in a dream more than a vision in a dream can give. . . . If ye come to tell of what ye have seen, make it plain that it was but a dream. See ye make it very plain. Give no poor fool pretext to think ye are claiming knowledge of what no mortal knows."

We must remember this in *All Hallows' Eve*. We may profit from the illuminations and stimulations of conjecture. We may take in-sight and strength from imaginative events and symbols that drama-tize for us doctrinal abstractions (remembering that Jesus himself never dealt in theological abstractions but always in parable and act). But we must remember the fallibility and inadequacy of hu-man imaginations and symbols.

On the other hand, something which is not at all the same thing as the subject of this warning is confused with it by some today. The primary heretical tendency of our age is the denial of the supernatural. If it tacitly permits God to be assumed as supernatural, it tries at the least to deny the intrusion of the supernatural into that tangible, manipulatable, circumscribed realm that we are accus-tomed to call the "natural." The current code word for this is "de-mythologizing." Williams is unyieldingly against it, though he did not live to see the movement penetrate the Church and seminaries deeply and find spokesmen among prelates.

"Natural" and "supernatural" are false categories except understood as convenient though risky terms for different levels of the complex nature of all Creation. I will use the words henceforth, without quotation marks, with natural understood as the world of time and of measurable physical phenomena observable and partly controllable by us, and supernatural understood as the dimensions of reality, the realm of God's power, beyond our present observation and comprehension, inaccessible to our unaided reach, and outside of time. The words "present observation and comprehension" are important. History is a process of expanding observation and comprehension of the Creation, through science and other means, and Christian thought regards this expansion as an aspect of God's continuing revelation and intention for us. We cannot know in advance how far God will carry that revelation in the course of mankind's earthly history. How fast it will unfold, how far into His purposes and ways it will enable us to see while in the flesh, time will tell to the ultimate generations. But we cannot doubt that if we grow in knowledge of His Creation and Himself we do so by His grace and will.

Such writers as George MacDonald, C. S. Lewis, J. R. R. Tolkien, Dorothy L. Sayers, T. S. Eliot, and others going back through a tradition that includes Goethe, Milton, and Dante, use the symbols of things and acts, in what is commonly (not very satisfactorily) called fantasy. A common thread among their diverse purposes is keeping us conscious of the supernatural, which means keeping us conscious of the omnipotence and omnipresence of God possibly more effectively than any other medium of story can do. C. S. Lewis remarks, in *The Screwtape Letters,* the way in which many of us have "eased the burden of intolerable strangeness which this universe imposes on us by dividing it into two halves (natural and supernatural) and encouraging the mind never to think of both in the same context." Williams unsparingly forces us to think of both in the same context continually, and some readers find this uncomfortable or unbearable. T. S. Eliot said, "Charles Williams was a man who was always able to live in the material and spiritual world at once, a man to whom the two worlds are equally real because they are one world."

Possibly it is not a complete, or adequate, comment upon the modern "demythologizing" trends in contemporary theological debate (which includes the so-called death-of-God theology), but it is certainly true that in a significant part these trends are a disbelieving drawing away from this two-worlds-in-one. To the intellectually honest, to pull away from that is to pull away from the whole Christian revelation. One may take Christianity or leave it, but one cannot separate it from the tremendous linked mystery of Creation-Incarnation-Resurrection-Ascension-Pentecost. In their theological fantasies, Williams, Lewis, and the other writers cited use imaginatively the symbols of this great mystery to freshen our awareness of that which so transcends us that much of it must be experienced and understood by us through symbols. Remember that symbol is a way of expressing truth—it does not denote something that is not true.

The Meaning of Images and Actions

Let us explore some of the meanings of the principal images and actions as we encounter them in the unfolding plot. The detail and subtlety of the book are so great that we cannot hope to touch all aspects. Also, like all writers, Williams is not consistently successful. There are things in the book that do not come off, that remain obscure, or otherwise fall short of his vision. Finally, we must allow for my own limitations, blindspots, and predilections as an interpreter.

The heroine (such nonfashionable categories are wholly appropriate to Williams' stories) is a young woman of twenty-five, named Lester Furnival, who has been married six months. As the story opens she is dead, standing on Westminster Bridge, only a few feet from the place on the Embankment where she has just been killed by the accidental crash of a fighter plane. Ironically, it is 1945 and the fighting has just ended although the formalities of peace have not been finished. The city around her is familiar but somehow ghostlike, empty. She sees her husband, Richard, approach, makes an involuntary gesture of warding him off as he reaches out to her, and then he seems to disappear. At this moment she begins to realize that she is dead.

Then she meets another dead girl, Evelyn, an almost-lifelong friend in the qualified sense that underlies many such nominal relationships. It was just that "she was sincerely used to Evelyn." They had been killed together, by an ironic circumstance. Evelyn, a whimperer and whiner, toward whom Lester feels brusquely impatient, tags along with the stronger girl through the empty streets of a London that is the same but different. As far as knowledgeable decision goes, their wandering is aimless. It's important to realize that time and space are no longer confines to these girls as they are to those characters of the story still alive in body. They are in the precincts of eternity, though this is realized slowly.

A month or so later, Richard Furnival visits his friend Jonathan Drayton, a painter. There he sees an unposed portrait of a man known as Simon the Clerk, a cultist with a growing following. The mother of Betty Wallingford, Jonathan's fiancée (though the mother does not consent to the engagement), is Simon's closest aide. Betty is caught in their sphere involuntarily. The portrait, which outrages Lady Wallingford, shows the Clerk with an expression of almost imbecilic concentrated emptiness, paradoxical though it sounds. His followers, pictured as massed and flowing into a rock cleft, seem like hordes of small beetles, and their Master like a great beetle.

Jonathan has painted another picture, a view of the heart of London in a dawnlike light. But the light has an arresting, ineffable quality, mysterious and perplexing both to others who look and to the artist himself. The painting changes during the story—slightly, subtly, but significantly—the mysterious quality of the light becoming more glorious and pronounced. Somehow Jonathan has captured unconsciously a glimpse of the eternal other City containing this city.

When Simon the Clerk sees his portrait, unlike Lady Wallingford he likes it and wishes Jonathan to paint him more. He is secretly fascinated by its intuitive penetration of his reality. But he dismisses the painting of London scornfully, suggesting it be discarded. ". . . hide it for a year, and come with me, and then look at it again, and you will see it as I do"—which is certainly true.

Simon is a magician, an adept, a cabalist. Cabala is a mystical occultism, of rabbinic development, medieval and even earlier in origin. It is not inherently evil, rooted as it is in scriptural mysticism, but can be used evilly by such as Simon, who presumably also goes beyond the cabalistic elements. His title, "clerk," signifies "cleric" or "clergyman," for he is a sort of diabolical priest whose followers call him "the Father."

The unknown facts are that, born in Paris in the eighteenth century, he is nearly two hundred years old, though his face is ageless. He has created magically and sent into the world two simulacra, images of himself that are not known to be such, types of artificial alter ego. One of them has developed a mass following in Russia, the other in China. Already in world politics there is a stirring demand that these "three" so-called spiritual leaders should meet to resolve the problems of the world. By that expedient the Clerk will gain political and spiritual domination. (Williams anticipated the triple sphere of world power as we now see it, just as in *Shadows of Ecstasy*, the first-written and least good of the novels, he anticipated a revolutionary, emergent Africa.)

Simon, again secretly, is the father of Betty Wallingford, who was conceived not in love and passion but in cold calculation for a diabolical use. She is about to be murdered, magically. She has often been sent, in a trance state, into that other City where Lester is wandering, to bring back information. But the Clerk needs a servant-informant there who is wholly, permanently in it. Lady Wallingford is a willing accomplice in all this.

Simon is a Jew, necessarily in the frame of this story, for "Only a Jew could utter the Jewish, which was the final, word of power." (Here, by implication, Hebrew is analogous to the "Old Solar," in C. S. Lewis's *Out of the Silent Planet* trilogy, a primal language of Creation.) As in Williams' *Many Dimensions* (an excellent book with which to begin reading him), the Tetragrammaton is the word of power, the JHVH (Jahweh) of the old Hebrew script written without vowels.

But though the demonic Simon, the villain, is a Jew, there is no slightest hint of anti-Semitism. That would be impossible to Williams' Old Testament-encompassing biblicism. Simon, like the earlier Simon Magus rebuffed by Peter, is simply a corrupt Jew, a Jewish Faustus. He is even a type of the anti-Christ. He is contrasted directly to another Jew, "Joseph ben David" (Jesus). Simon, magically prolonging his life, "had refused the possibilities of death. He would not go to it, as that other child of a Jewish girl had done. That other had refused safeguard and miracle; he had refused the achievement of security. He had gone into death—and the Clerk supposed it his failure—as the rest of mankind go—ignorant and in pain. The Clerk had set himself to decline pain and ignorance. So that now he had not any capacities but those he could himself gain." He has, in part, embraced the temptations which Christ rejected in the wilderness. The melodrama of the book is concerned with the effort on both the "natural" and "supernatural" levels to save Betty from the clutches of the Clerk. Jonathan and Lester are the chief operatives on these respective levels; but as the "supernatural" is the most profound, it is Lester's efforts that are most crucial. Significantly, she understands only slightly more than Jonathan and Richard what this is all about, until almost the end.

The deeper, subtler thread of story involves Lester's adjustment to her new existence and gradual movement from the lesser city toward the greater one. It is a form of Pilgrim's progress. The means of her growth or advancement is her instinctive, disinterested desire to meet the need of Betty when, by chance and uncomprehendingly, she finds herself standing by at a moment crucial in the Clerk's machinations upon Betty. Later she extends this willingness to give, and to bear, even to the unresponsive Evelyn.

As Betty is called back from the brink of death by Lester's uncomprehending but willing intercession, the living girl herself begins a spiritual progress, growing in radiant joy. At the end, willing to substitute herself even unto death if need be, she has acquired the spiritual energy to heal once more, by holy power, the poor souls whom the Clerk had falsely healed by magic and who, upon his downfall, have lapsed back into their sufferings. She is drained by this task, and as she is now ready to enter into her shared life with Jonathan, we expect that though she will know confident serenity, she will not dwell constantly, in the worldly city, on the high spiritual level she had attained briefly. But Lester, leaving the purgatorial shadows of the former world behind, now moves permanently from the mere "precincts of felicity" into that full radiance glimpsed in part in Jonathan's painting.

Operative in saving Betty also is the "wise water," the holy water, consecrated solely by the intention, with which a loving nurse, in secret defiance of Lady Wallingford, had baptized the child. Water has further symbolic significance in the story. The rain in the other City (perplexing to the Clerk) and the rain that in the climactic scenes accompanies the downfall of the Clerk, penetrating his dwelling and dissolving his magical creations, is also holy water, "wise water," the Living Water of Christ.

Evelyn's story is a counterpoint to the spiritual enlargement of Lester, in one world, and of Betty, Jonathan, and Richard in another. A wise priest once remarked that probably no one would be in Hell except those who were absolutely determined to be there. Unfortunately Evelyn—though it is not misfortune but choice that damns her—is determined to be there. Doggedly, frantically, she resists and fights any call to larger being. She will not face the unknowns of spiritual growth but clings to false, cozy-seeming assurances, to petty, malicious, possessive pleasures.

The saddest comment on Evelyn is Betty's relief, even gladness, that the girl is dead—a gladness and relief that are not malicious but simple expressions of release from an oppression. Williams speaks of "the terror and the despair of those of the dead who, passing from this world, leave only that just relief behind. That which should go with them—the goodwill of those they have known —does not. . . . To go with no viaticum but this relief is a very terrible thing. . . . The whole City—ghostly or earthly" felt it. "Disburdened, it rejoiced. . . ."

Lester and Evelyn both are true types. We may be like one or the other.

The heart and essence of the book are expressed in Lester's late-achieved, superimposed vision of layers and layers of the city of London. She has glimpses of it at many points in time, even to the open country before the city was there. All these are simultaneous and coinhere in "London." In turn, London coinheres with all other earthly cities and with the City of God, of which the cities of men are dim, imperfect images—yet actual images, as each man is a dim, imperfect, yet actual, image of God.

Yet all she saw, and did not quite wonder at seeing, was but a small part of the whole. There around her lay not only London, but all cities— coincident yet each distinct; or else, in another mode, lying by each other as the districts of one city lie. She could, had she the time and her occasions permitted, have gone to any she chose—any time and place that men had occupied or would occupy. There was no huge metropolis in which she would have been lost, and no single village which would itself have been lost in all that contemporaneous mass. In this City lay all—London and New York, Athens and Chicago, Paris and Rome and Jerusalem; it was that to which they led in the lives of their citizens. When her time came, she would know what lay behind the high empty façades of her early experience of death; it was necessary that she should first have been compelled to linger among those façades, for till she had waited there and till she had known the first grace of a past redeemed into love, she could not bear even a passing glimpse of that civil vitality. For here citizenship meant relationship and knew it; its citizens lived new acts or lived the old at will. What on earth is only in the happiest moments of friendship or love was now normal. Lester's new friendship with Betty was but the merest flicker, but it was that flicker which now carried her soul. (Pp. 188-89.)

The other major theme, substituted love, is merely glanced at in the phrase "For here citizenship meant relationship and knew it." The epitomizing historic act of substituted love was the Incarnation with the subsequent Passion of Christ. The truest, most comprehensive imitation of Christ is in the willing and carrying out of the substitution by free, unreserved gift of oneself to carry the trial, burden, pain, temptation, or punishment of another. That is the central theme of Williams' novel immediately preceding this one, *Descent Into Hell,* in which the point is developed that such substitution of love is not limited by space or by time, backward or forward.

Mysteriously, perplexingly, there is not always a context that permits this great substitution. One must seize the chance as it comes in the flow of events. Lester stumbles upon it at the bedside of the almost dead Betty and acts without understanding much beyond her loving intention. More deliberately, she tries it again when she consents to enter with Evelyn the grotesque clay image made by the Clerk, but the offering is refused by Evelyn. Betty is prepared to make it in the climactic scene, but what Williams calls "the Acts of the City" do not require it of her, and she gives of herself, instead, short of unto the death, to the despairing followers of the false Father who now need a true healing.

Having taken a general survey of the story and its principal elements, together with a glance at the general frame and implication of Williams' thought, we can now take a closer look at certain details. Again it is necessary to say that a great deal will remain untouched, unremarked.

Williams' "City" is the City of God, in the primary sense of the Apocalypse of St. John: ". . . and I John saw the holy city . . . descending out of heaven from God, having the glory of God. . . ." He discusses this in more conventional apologetical terms in his book

He Came Down From Heaven, but it is much more rewarding in the novels, except for any unfortunate people who, forgetting Jesus, persuade themselves that story is an inferior medium, less "learned," "scholarly," or "deep" than more didactic forms. I do not say that to denigrate the latter (for better or worse such an essay as this is of that kind, and I confess I would be happier to be engaged in the former). Lewis, Williams, Sayers, Eliot, and MacDonald all wrote well and often in direct argument, but these are really backups, or extended reflections, on their principal expressions, analogous to the relation between Bernard Shaw's plays and prefaces.

The Johannine City is also the source of Augustine's *City of God.* It is the New Jerusalem, and is also the Sarras of the Arthurian Grail Legend, of which Williams has written in his mystical poems, *Taliessin Through Logres,* and *The Region of the Summer Stars.* In *All Hallows' Eve* there is a special, localized value to the term "city" as applied to actual, secular London, for to Londoners that denotes not greater London, but the city's heart, encompassing St. Paul's as well as that most worldly of power concentrations, London's financial district.

The central statement on the substitution of love occurs in the course of Lester's chance presence at Betty's bedside as Simon the Clerk is about to produce her death magically. By spontaneous impulse of her spirit, Lester interposes herself. As the malign spell threatens to engulf her instead of Betty, she feels herself mystically supported on a frame, which is the image of the Cross (another and constantly available substitution). Afterward,

oblivion took her. The task was done, and repose is in the rhythm of that world, and some kind of knowledge of sleep, since as a baby the Divine Hero closed his astonishing eyes, and his mother by him, and the princely Joseph, their young protector. Lester had taken the shock of the curse—no less willingly or truly that she had not known what she was doing. She had suffered instead of Betty, as Betty had once suffered through her; but the endurance had been short and the restoration soon, so quickly had the Name which is the City sprung to the rescue of its own. (P. 164.)

Do not overlook the penitential element in this substitution of love. One of Lester's tasks in the purgatorial experience is the working out and completing of that "love and charity with your neighbors" in which none of us can be wholly perfect as we approach the

Eucharist. There are other tasks for the dead, too, some of restoration, and some of disentanglement.

Lester's progress, her gradually increasing certainty of way (in contrast to Evelyn's floundering and sinking), is not a thing given to her for nothing, but a thing bought by effort. She wants to cling to the past. Her early thought of her husband, Richard, is a wish that "he should be there with her, prisoner with her, prisoner to her. If only he too would die, and come!" This possessiveness, entangled with and sometimes mistaken for love, has an echo of Milton's Eve, in *Paradise Lost,* after she has eaten the fruit. First she vacillates between inviting Adam to eat and be her equal in new powers and an impulse to keep an upper hand over him. Then another thought strikes Eve:

> . . . but what if God have seen,
> And death ensue? Then I shall be no more;
> And Adam, wedded to another Eve,
> Shall live with her enjoying, I extinct!
> A death to think! Confirmed, then, I resolve
> Adam shall share with me in bliss or woe.

In that determination, the fear of woe is the ruling impulse.

When Lester becomes aware that Betty is crying, within the magician's house, she is tempted to do nothing. "Betty must really learn to stand up for herself. 'Must she indeed?' Lester's own voice said to her. She exclaimed, with the fervent habit of her mortality: 'Hell!'" There is her choice. To turn away from this felt need because of weariness or wariness of what it might involve would be a choice Hell-directed. Evelyn, standing by, calls petulantly, "Oh, come *away!*" Then, "At the words Lester, for the first time in her life, saw a temptation precisely as it is when it has ceased to tempt —repugnant, implausible, mean." She enters the house. It is the choice that determines her direction and growth.

At this stage, "She was young in death, and the earth and its habits were, for this brief time, even more precious to her than they had been." At the same time, the lonely Richard, longing to affirm his love to Lester, mindful of shortcomings, errors, sins of their marriage, "submitted to memory, and in some poignant sense to a primitive remorse, for he was not yet spiritually old enough to repent." Both he and she grow into the knowledge of love as "a union of having and not-having, or else something different and beyond both. It was a kind of way of knowledge, and that knowledge perfect in its satisfaction." It is granted to them to reaffirm love mutually, and to part without clinging on either side, to meet once more in distant due course.

With Betty, even more than Lester, we find the Divine Mercy protecting its own. She is innocently manipulated by evil persons for evil ends. She is sent out from her body to walk in those precincts where Lester is, a reconnaissance instrument for the Clerk on brief missions until such time as he shall have her based there permanently under his thrall.

She read the future, but the future was not known to her; it was saved, by the redemption that worked in that place, for the master who had sent her there. Let him make his profit of it; her salvation was his peril. The activities and judgments of the world in that new January were recorded in her, but she, being magically commanded, was yet free. (Pp. 83-84.)

Free, that is, of the guilt of willing complicity.

There is ironic, dramatic foreshadowing, in the fact that the Clerk cannot find his name mentioned in the not very distant future newspapers he scans through her. Though this perplexes and disquiets him, his fatal confidence in his powers blinds him to its true meaning.

An important element in the protection of Betty is the baptism, performed by her nurse without the knowledge of the evil parents. Betty has long had a mysterious dream-vision of "the wise water." She felt herself, as a child, immersed in the depths of a lake. A great fish (one of the classical Christ symbols, from the Greek *Ichthys* [fish], which is an acrostic for the Greek phrase "Jesus Christ, the Son of God, the Savior") lifts her to the sunny surface of the lake, whence she is taken by her nurse, who says, "There, dearie, no-one can undo that; bless God for it."

Betty and Jonathan track down this vision to its simpler reality by finding and visiting the old nurse. Williams sums up:

And now as in some tales Merlin had by the same Rite issued from the womb in which he had been mysteriously conceived, so this child of magic had been after birth saved from magic by a mystery, beyond magic. The natural affection of this woman . . . had in fact dispelled the shadows of giant schemes. And this then was what that strange Rite called baptism was—a state of being of which water was the material identity, a life rippling and translucent with joy. (P. 208.)

As the Holy Spirit will protect, he will also take what we do and perfect it—as we can never do. The nurse expresses it:

. . . one afternoon in the nursery, I got the water and I prayed God to bless it, though I don't know now how I dared, and I marked you with it, and said the Holy Name, and I thought: "Well, I can't get the poor dear godfathers and godmothers, but the Holy Ghost'll be her godfather and I'll do what I can." (Pp. 207-8.)

"I'll do what I can" is the governing principle of Christian behavior. It underlies the Collect phrase "for without Thee we are not able to please Thee." It is touched again when Betty is wandering on her disembodied errand. She reflects: "Someone had once told her that her mind wasn't very strong, 'and indeed it isn't,' she thought gaily, 'but it's quite strong enough to do what it's got to do, and what it hasn't got to do it needn't worry about not doing.'"

There is an indication, so casual that it may be overlooked, that Betty is naturally of a higher spiritual power than Lester. After the magician's spell has been thwarted, literally deflected, turned aside, Lester looks at her and "knew at once that a greater than she was here." Yet we cannot live, especially in the contexts of the full stream of the world, always on a height of spiritual elevation. We are told of Betty:

That free and (as it were) immaculate self which had been by high disposition granted her was bound now to take on the conditions of its earthly place and natural heredity. The miracle that had preserved her was over, and she too must be subjected to the tribulations and temptations of common life. (P. 230.)

[Lester, on her part] was bound to pass more wholly into that other world which cannot catch its true and perfect union with this until the resurrection of all the past; the occasional resurrection which then obtained for her was rather purgatorial than paradisal, though sometimes the two were simply one. (P. 230.)

At the end, after the Clerk has been destroyed by the backward rush upon himself of all his evil projections, Lester breaks the earthly ties, joins with all the other blessed hallows. "The tremor of brightness received her."

The purgatorial theme finds its fullest statement in Williams' description of those precincts in which the newly dead girls are wandering, and into which Betty is dispatched on errands:

> It lay there, as it always does—itself offering no barriers, open to be trodden, ghostly to this world and to heaven, and in its upper reaches ghostly also to those in its lower reaches where (if at all) hell lies. It is ours and not ours, for men and women were never meant to dwell there long; though it is held by some that certain unaccountable disappearances have been into that world, and that a few (even living) may linger there awhile. But mostly these streets are only for the passing through of the newly dead. It is not for human bodies, though it has known a few— "Enoch, Elijah, and the Lady"—though they not in London, but, in the places where they died. (P. 77.)

In reading the continuation of this passage in Chapter Four of the book itself, observe the interesting, poignant reflection of England's and London's suffering in the war, and the speculation that perhaps, indeed, the city perished.

The sheer occultism, which supplies the melodrama, deserves some comment. We do not have to take any of it literally, or believe any of its manifestations. What we must believe—if we are Christians, and maybe even if we are not—is the reality of the will to evil and the corruption of the inherently good through the operation of that will. There is an ancient tradition both in Christian and non-Christian contexts behind the details of the Clerk's operations, which Williams builds up brilliantly, perhaps in almost too much detail.

One of Williams' recurring themes in the novels is the attempt of wicked men to subvert the inherent power in holy things. In *Many Dimensions* it is a cube of the Original Matter with the Tetragrammaton at its heart. In *War in Heaven* it is the Holy Grail. In *All Hallows' Eve,* after all the lesser spells and occult techniques, the ultimate word of power which the Clerk rashly dares to pervert is the Tetragrammaton.

Exhibited through Simon and his works is the difference between magic and grace. Magic is a direct operation, from without, upon the person or thing that is its object. Grace is a resource of power, operative in any case only when the will, by free choice, reaches out toward or opens itself to it. Simon knows nothing of grace, but its Providential operation is sufficient to undo all his works.

He misuses not only that ultimate Name, the Tetragrammaton.

He abuses other words that we see abused daily around us in everything from politics, to commerce, to personal relationships.

He came near her [Betty]; he spoke over her—he had a very great courage —those august words: "peace, joy, love." He used them for what he needed, and they meant to him—and to her—what he chose. . . . He wished her to be an instrument only; *peace, joy, love,* were but names for the passivity of the instrument. He was unique; yet he was no more than any man—only raised to a higher power and loosed in himself. (Pp. 73-74.)

Williams must have read widely in the Midrashic lore of cabala and Jewish demon tales. The grotesque dwarf woman whom Simon makes to house the spirit of Evelyn, and into whom Lester enters with her, is known in Jewish lore as a *golem.* The word denotes a lifeless image shaped from dust, clay, and other matter, to which life is imparted by cabalistic rites culminating in the pronouncing of the Tetragrammaton. Further general information on this, with two traditional *golem* tales, can be found on pages 603-612 of *A Treasury of Jewish Folklore* (New York: Crown Publishers, 1948), edited by Nathan Ausubel.

Simon is not a devil, but a man. He functions demonically, diabolically, as in varying degrees do all who corrupt what is good and especially those who pervert what is holy. Simon believes Jesus had failed by going to death—as indeed even the wavering Disciples had been tempted to believe until they saw their resurrected Master. We may ask, would not such a learned adept of supernatural mysteries as Simon have known the truth? Significantly, there are kinds of knowledge, and motives to pursue such knowledge, which will close off from us other and more essential knowledge. In pursuit of knowledge unto damnation, Simon took the path directly away from knowledge unto salvation. The Tree of Knowledge was always perilous to man. He came to believe, "You are different; you are not under the law; you are particular," which, in one of the greatest realistic novels of good and evil, was the undoing of Dostoyevsky's Raskolnikov, in *Crime and Punishment.*

Do we run into the problem of total depravity with Simon? There are still in him the vestiges of good qualities: courage (becoming temerity), austere dedication to purpose (becoming obsession), immense learning and discipline (becoming pride), the performing of works of healing (from perverted motives). He was no more evil once than any other man, but consciously, cumulatively he chose evil until he reached something like total depravity in the sense of passing beyond his own capacity to change, retract, and repent before his own acts undo him.

Williams has done something interesting with Lady Wallingford. She is as evil a woman and unnatural a mother as literature can offer. She has unsexed herself, she is willing in effect to dash out her babe's brains, in the terms of Lady Macbeth's horrible invocation to black powers to possess her. Yet also like Lady Macbeth, she has done her deeds in part from her own sort of love for the man to whom she is committed—it happens in Lady Wallingford's case to be an adulterous as well as ambitious bond.

One would expect scant mercy or grace for her. She would seem a real temptation to yield to the notion of total depravity. But grace is patient and will go a long way with a little. She commits an accidental substitution, not of love, in the climactic rites of the desperate Clerk. By accident her blood permeates the doll-like image which was designed to recapture Betty. The Clerk cannot stop the process, and is as callous about his primary lieutenant as about everyone and everything else. It seems as if this will be the death of Lady Wallingford, but falls short of that due to the dissolving of the spells by the holy rain. She is left alive, but senseless, helpless. But even in this burnt-out case, Williams tells us of possibilities—not easy certainties, but possibilities.

She had given herself away and her self would be no longer there, or rather (as if it were a new-born child) would have to be cared for and trained afresh. But since in that gift she had desired the good of another and not her own, since she had indeed willed to give her self, the City secluded her passion and took her gift to its own divine self. She had, almost in a literal physical sense, to be born again; at least she had to grow again, and over the growth her daughter was to preside. That tenderness was to meet her needs, and (if she could ever speak) to answer her stumbling words. She was now almost in that state to which her master had willed to reduce their child; the substitution was one of the Acts of the City. Her spiritual knowledge lay unconscious, as it were in the depth of the separating and uniting waters; her body under the common sun. Resurrection must be from the very beginning and meanwhile Betty was to do for her mother, while she lived, all that love could do. (Pp. 270-71.)

Williams has evoked some of the most frightful and modernly sophisticated images of damnation, but he has never forgotten to link them with the most profound reminders of the Christian promises of hope, and the patience and power of redemptive purpose. It is appropriate that Simon the Clerk meets his dreadful, grotesquely self-induced end on All Hallows' Eve—a grim Hallowe'en story—when by tradition the evil spirits are abroad with the good. From that climax the story modulates naturally into the blessedness and light of All Saints'.

Again we must remember not to take Williams' images of that other world, or City, as literal truths about things which he could not know. (Ironically, soon after finishing the book he died, entering into the true knowledge of the City not long after his fictitious Lester did so in his book. He was dead before the All Hallows' Eve of 1945, to which he had projected the climax of his story.) The value of his instructive symbolic fantasy is that, as Betty said about Jonathan's painting of the light of the City, "It's terribly like a fact" in its vision of the nature of man and the multiple dimensions of the reality he inhabits.

Till We Have Faces

An Introduction and Commentary

> As Thou
> Art jealous, Lord, so I am jealous now,
> Thou lovest not, till from loving more, thou free
> My soul: Whoever gives, takes liberty.
>
> —*John Donne*

To THOUSANDS of people in England and America, the discovery of C. S. Lewis has been a momentous experience, akin to Keats's first reading of Chapman's Homer. His writing not only opened old worlds of Christian belief all too often unexplored but also created new ones of unimagined richness and power through his mastery of theological exposition and mythical narrative. He was not only an eloquent Christian and a fashioner of breathtaking fantasies but also a scholar and teacher of great eminence; in short, a man of prodigious learning coupled with vaulting imagination. His novel *Till We Have Faces* is considered by many critics his finest narrative, and it marks a radical departure from his others in subject matter, form, and style. A re-creation of the classical myth of Cupid and Psyche in highly original terms, it is a picture of a heathenish world—dark, fanatical, and barbarous, yet also illumined by an abiding if abrasive love.

About the Author

Clive Staples Lewis was born on November 29, 1898, in Belfast, Ireland, the second son of Albert James Lewis, a solicitor of Welsh extraction, and Flora Augusta Hamilton, of Irish and English blood. His older brother, Warren, an officer in the regular army and historian of the French *ancien régime*, was his lifelong companion and devoted helper. The two boys spent much time together. On rainy days they had the run of a large, rambling house, and let their imaginations roam free with paint and pencil, creating a fanciful "Animal-land" and a country named Boxen. Lewis's early schooling was not very happy. A boy of sensitive disposition, turned somewhat to melancholy by the early death of his mother and by the rather inelastic temperament of his father, Lewis found the schools he attended gloomy houses of detention. The first one, presided over by a headmaster later certified insane, he named "Belsen" in his autobiographical study, *Surprised by Joy*. After asking his father to withdraw him from a later one, Malvern College, he studied privately with W. T. Kirkpatrick, a man of ruthlessly logical mind and a very stimulating teacher. It was Kirkpatrick who first recognized Lewis's literary ability. He had actually been trying to write since the age of seven: histories, stories, poems, and fantasies of "Animal-land" and Boxen. When almost thirteen, he wrote a complete novel. All of this writing was stimulated by voracious reading. His discovery of the fantasies of George Macdonald made a deep impression on him, as did the works of Chaucer, Malory, Scott, the romantic poets, and William Morris. At about the age of fourteen he first came in contact with the *Nibelungenlied* and the Norse sagas. They were the source of what he called his "Northernness," a Germanic strain which, he maintained, was more important to him than any Celticism.

In 1916 he won a classical scholarship to University College, Oxford, and began his residence the following year. After service in the Officers' Training Corps of the university, he was commissioned lieutenant in the Somerset Light Infantry, and reached the western front on his birthday in 1917. The following April he was wounded; and before he had fully recovered, the war ended. After being demobilized, he returned to Oxford and had a brilliant career as a scholar, winning a double "First": in "Greats," 1922, and in English, 1923. His achievement in these two fields won him a tutorial appointment at University College in 1924, and in the next year a fellowship at Magdalen, a post which he held until 1954. He rapidly became known as an extraordinarily stimulating teacher; his lectures were always crowded. His warm, gregarious personality, his delight in the snap and crackle of male disputation, and his prodigious learning (easily worn), made him one of the liveliest members of a group which met periodically for the discussion of literature, or any other subject which seemed important: J. R. R. Tolkien, Roy Campbell, John Wain, Lord David Cecil, Charles Williams, and Fr. Gervase Mathew, among others. Very often their meeting place was an Oxford pub called The Eagle and The Child, commonly known as The Bird and Baby. As this American visitor can testify, Lewis was the animating catalyst at these meetings. He was a superb talker and a good listener.

In 1953 Lewis, who had never married, met Joy Davidman Gresham, an American woman who had been converted to Anglicanism largely through his influence. They were married in 1957, although Joy was at that time in the hospital, an apparently doomed victim of cancer. At first the marriage was largely one of convenience—a means of allowing Joy to remain in England permanently. Soon, however, it developed into deep love, with Lewis completely enthralled by his wife's brilliant mind and keen wit. Her death on June 13, 1960, was a terrible blow, poignantly described in *A Grief Observed*. At the time, Lewis was professor of medieval and Renaissance literature at Cambridge, a post to which he had been appointed in 1954. His health, however, had been failing for some years, and in October, 1963, he felt obliged to resign his position. This transatlantic traveler saw him at about that time and found him in good spirits and, to all appearances, in sound physical condition. A month later, however, on November 22, the day of President Kennedy's assassination, he collapsed and died. A double disaster indeed!

Lewis left a rich legacy. Apart from his brilliant teaching, he made lasting contributions in the fields of fiction, literary scholarship, and popular theology. There is no need to give an elaborate account of his writings; it is enough to note certain ones which are representative of his wide range of interests: in fiction, the planetary novels *Out of the Silent Planet* (1938), *Perelandra* (1943), and *That Hideous Strength* (1945), the seven books for children about the mythical land of Narnia (1950-56), and of course *Till We Have Faces* (1956); in literary scholarship, *The Allegory of Love* (1936), *A Preface to Paradise Lost* (1941), and

English Literature in the Sixteenth Century (1954); and in popular theology, *The Screwtape Letters* (1942), *Miracles* (1947), and *Mere Christianity* (1952). During the Second World War, he became widely known for a series of radio talks on Christian religion. He did this not only with great dialectic skill but also with the zeal of the convert. Though he was brought up as an Anglican, he forswore Christianity at the age of fourteen and considered himself henceforth an atheist. Like Francis Thompson, however, he was pursued by an untiring God. He finally surrendered to Christianity in 1931, while on a bus trip with his brother to Whipsnade Zoo. Ever after, he was unquestionably the most eminent and influential Anglican layman in the world. Most of his books, he once replied to one of his critics, were evangelistic, whether overtly, like *Pilgrim's Regress* (his early narrative of a spiritual quest), *Reflections on the Psalms, The Abolition of Man,* and *The Great Divorce;* or tangentially, as in the trilogy of novels, the Narnia books, the autobiographical *Surprised by Joy,* and *Till We Have Faces.* Even his scholarly works were impregnated with the Christian tradition, and his letters to his friends are filled with theological discussion. In a lesser man all this might seem to imply a solemn weightiness of religious fervor, difficult to transmit and somewhat overpowering to receive. Nothing could be further from the truth. Lewis was the most elastic and buoyant of writers; like his Elwin Ransom, the hero of the trilogy, especially at the end of *That Hideous Strength,* Lewis verily seems a high union of body and spirit—flesh suffused with heavenly joy.

Introduction to the Book

The subtitle of *Till We Have Faces* is "A Myth Retold"; and Lewis is at some pains, in a letter to Fr. Peter Milward, to say what he means by myth, especially as opposed to allegory. Although he said on one occasion that no man could write a story in which another man could not find an allegory, he had no allegorical intention in *Till We Have Faces.* The characters in it are not supposed to represent abstract qualities, as do the people in *Pilgrim's Progress* or *The Faerie Queene.* "A good myth," says Lewis, "(i.e. a story out of which ever varying meanings will grow for different readers and in different ages) is a higher thing than an allegory (into which *one* meaning has been put). Into an allegory a man can put only what he already knows; in a myth he puts what he does not yet know and could not come by in any other way."[1]

In *An Experiment in Criticism,* he goes into detail as to the characteristics of myth. In the first place, it is extraliterary in that its value depends not on its appearance in any literary work, not on the fact that great classical writers may have told it, but on its independent power. It depends hardly at all on suspense or surprise; its movement is inevitable. Further, myth relies little on human sympathy; we do not project ourselves strongly into the characters; they seem to move in another world. (This seems an overstatement when considering *Till We Have Faces.*) Myth stresses the fantastic, the impossible, and the preternatural. It may be sad or joyful, but it is always grave; a comic myth is impossible. Finally, it is not only grave but also awe-inspiring; it has a numinous quality, that is, an awareness of divine and spiritual things. The myth, therefore, seems to range independently at a high level, developing moral force inevitably from its own existence rather than from the intention of the author. Lewis once said to a group of friends that he had never started a story with the idea of a moral or message. "The story itself should force its moral upon you. You find out what the moral is by writing the story."[2] The mythical, or fantastic, story, he said, has a generalized power even while it remains concrete. It aims to "present in palpable form not concepts or even experiences but whole classes of experience, and to throw off irrelevancies. But at its best it can do more; it can give us experiences we have never had and thus, instead of 'commenting on life,' can add to it."[3]

The story of *Till We Have Faces* is told by Orual, eldest of the three daughters of King Trom of Glome, a small barbaric state on the outer edge of the ancient Greek world. Her own mother is dead, and Trom has married a second time and has had a daughter, Istra. Orual's Greek mentor, Lysias, nicknamed the Fox, says that the Greek form of Istra's name is Psyche. From infancy, Istra has been extraordinarily beautiful and seems to have the capacity of shedding beauty on commonplace objects around her. Orual, on the other hand, is very ill-favored, so much so that eventually she wears a heavy veil to hide her face. A drought and a plague devastate the land, and the priest of the goddess Ungit, whose representation is a block of ugly, shapeless stone, decides that a human sacrifice must be offered in propitiation. Psyche is chosen and is taken to the top of the Grey Mountains, where she is chained to a tree. There she is to become the bride of the Shadowbrute, who is either Ungit herself or Ungit's son, the god of the mountain.

Orual grieves over Psyche's fate and finally, with a loyal soldier, Bardia, goes secretly to the mountaintop to bury Psyche's bones, if she can find them. But she finds no bones; instead she discovers Psyche herself, in a beautiful spot on the farther side of the mountain. Psyche explains that after she had been chained to the tree, the west wind carried her away to a place where a splendid palace was given to her, and where she is visited nightly by a husband who forbids her to see his face. The palace, invisible to all eyes save Psyche's, is at the very spot where they are standing. On hearing this unbelievable tale, Orual determines that her sister must be out of her mind and that she must rescue her, despite her radiant joy over her new condition. But Psyche refuses to be persuaded, and Orual and Bardia sadly return to the city. Before they do so, however, Orual, for an instant, beholds the palace which Psyche has described to her.

Badly shaken, Orual is convinced by Bardia and the Fox that some evil has befallen Psyche, and she returns to the mountain, either to rescue her sister or to kill her and herself. Again, however, Psyche refuses to return to Glome. Desperately, Orual wounds herself in the arm with her dagger. To save her from suicide, Psyche agrees to light a lamp to see her husband's face that night when he comes to her bed. Orual watches, and at last sees a light. Immediately a great storm arises, and a man with a beautiful face tells Orual that Psyche must wander sorrowing over the world. Her anguished cries gradually fade in the distance. Profoundly shaken, Orual returns to Glome.

After the death of her father, she becomes queen of Glome, a dedicated and successful ruler, suppressing as well as she can her sorrow over the fate of Psyche. Under the instruction of her faithful Bardia, she even becomes a skillful swordsman and kills the invading Prince Argan of Phars in a formal duel. Many years go by; the kingdom of Glome prospers, though Orual always harbors a great bitterness in her heart. As an old woman she happens on a little forest temple dedicated to Psyche. On hearing from the priest what she considers false or misleading versions of the story of Psyche, she decides to write her own. The rest of the novel is a series of harrowing dreams or visions, which shadow forth Orual's agonized approach to understanding of her sin and her final release from its burden. The first revelation comes when she realizes, to her horror, that she and the goddess Ungit, "that all-devouring, womblike, yet barren, thing," are one and the same. Then she has other visions: terrible tasks are laid upon her, one of them requiring her to burrow deep into the earth; and in another she walks over burning sands and up a mountain to find the water of death, only to discover herself before the court of the gods, presenting her complaint. Finally, she realizes that she has no valid case against the gods, and asks the central question of the novel, so appropriate to a person who has veiled herself for many years: How can the gods meet men until men have faces—that is, until men present themselves as they really are, without pretense? The spirit of Lysias the Fox then leads her into a chamber whose walls are covered with living stories, the greatest of which is Psyche's trip to the Deadlands to bring beauty from Death to Orual. Psyche returns with the casket of beauty and gives it to her sister, who abases herself before Psyche and acknowledges that her former love for her had been selfish. At this point the god of the mountain, the Shadowbrute, appears, and Orual finds herself transformed into beauty. "You are Psyche," says a great voice. So the gods judge. And Orual finds it possible to speak the truth at last, before she dies.

Discussion of the Themes

In the main, Lewis follows Apuleius's original narrative in *Metamorphoses*. Yet with what a world of difference! To the original rather objective tale is added the tension of almost unendurable personal conflict and decision. The whole story as told by Lewis, therefore, is an extraordinarily subtle tale of a person's lifelong attempt to achieve release from the burden of sin. And sin it is, in Orual's dogged determination to have full possession of her sister's heart. This is really the central issue of the story—a frightening exposition of the dangers of an enveloping love.

According to Walter Hooper, the editor of Lewis's poems, *Till We Have Faces* was begun as a poem but was never finished. Though written as prose fiction, it is infused, as so many of his narratives are, with the magnificent energy of the poetic imagination. In *The Allegory of Love*, Lewis makes a telling statement about poetry: "For poetry to spread its wings fully, there must be, besides the believed religion, a marvellous that knows itself as myth."[4] In *Till We Have Faces*, this poetic fusion of the religious and the marvellous is abundantly evident. The supernatural wonders of the myth of Cupid and Psyche are re-created in pictures of breathtaking beauty and power. The book is suffused, moreover, with a sense of "believed religion"— not Christian, to be sure, but certainly not incompatible with it. Not only the ethical issues which face Orual but also the mystery of the numinous, of faith (or lack of it) in the gods, of one's obligation to divinity—all these are part of the very texture of the book. It would indeed be hard to imagine Lewis writing on any subject without doing so in the context of religious belief.

Though it describes a pagan world, *Till We Have Faces* is a revelation of issues fundamental to Christian faith. Lewis discusses some of the most important of these in a letter to Professor Clyde S. Kilby on February 10, 1957:

An author doesn't necessarily understand the meaning of his own story better than anyone else, so I give my account of *Till We Have Faces* simply for what it is worth. The "levels" I am conscious of are these.

(1) A work of (supposed) historical imagination. A guess of what it might have been like in a little barbarous state on the borders of the Hellenistic world of Greek culture, just beginning to affect it. Hence the change from the old priest (of a very normal fertility mother-goddess) to Arnom; Stoic allegorisations of the myths standing to the original cult rather as Modernism to Christianity (but this is a parallel not an allegory). Much that you take as allegory was intended solely as realistic detail. The wagonmen are nomads from the steppes.

The children made mud pies not for symbolic purposes but because children do. The Pillar Room is simply a room. The Fox is such an educated Greek slave as you might find at a barbarous court—and so on.

(2) Psyche is an instance of the *anima naturaliter christiana* making the best of the Pagan religion she is brought up in and thus being guided (but always "under the cloud," always in terms of her own imaginations or that of her people) towards the true God. She is in some ways like Christ because every good man or woman is like Christ. What else could they be like? But of course my interest is primarily in Orual.

(3) Orual is [not a symbol] but an instance, a "case" of human affection in its natural condition, true, tender, suffering, but in the long run tyranically [*sic*] possessive and ready to turn to hatred when the beloved ceases to be its possession. What such love particularly cannot stand is to see the beloved passing into a sphere where it cannot follow. All this I hoped would stand as a mere story in its own right. But—

(4) Of course I had always in mind its close parallel to what is probably happening at this moment in at least five families in your home town. Someone becomes a Christian, or in a family nominally Christian already, does something like becoming a missionary or entering a religious order. The others suffer a sense of outrage. What they love is being taken from them. The boy must be mad. And the conceit of him! Or: is there something in it after all? Let's hope it is only a phase! If only he had listened to his natural advisers. Oh come back, come back, be sensible, be the dear son we used to know! Now I, as a Christian, have a good deal of sympathy with those jealous, suffering, puzzled people (for they do suffer, and out of their suffering much of the bitterness against religion arises). I believe the thing is common. There is very nearly a touch of it in Luke II.38, "Son, *why hast thou* so dealt with us?" And is the reply easy for a loving heart to bear?[5]

As Lewis indicates in this passage, he was trying to tell a tale of a damaging love which he "hoped would stand as a mere story in its own right." Yet, as he points out, it is also one with deep Christian implications. Lewis deals principally with the difference between love as devotion and love as possession. Further, he explores the mysterious duality of our concept of the divine, the source of all good and of power so great that it often invokes terror. He also deals with death in the symbolic sense, as an awakening to truth before the death of the body, and, finally, he strongly suggests the Christian longing for the reward of Heaven.

Orual's enveloping love for Psyche is an offense both to her sister and to the gods. In his treatise *Four Loves*, Lewis emphasizes the dangers of selfish loving. The mother who wants to do everything for her children, who insists on waiting up until they come in at night, is not only an infernal nuisance but a destructive influence as well. In the same work, Lewis carries this idea into the theological realm: "We may give our human loves the unconditional allegiance which we owe only to God. Then they become gods: then they become demons."[6] Though he does not say so explicitly, Lewis regards Orual's passion for her sister as an avaricious dehumanization, regarding a person as an object, a thing to be used for one's own gratification rather than an independent spirit. It is hardly necessary to indicate how contrary this is to the concept of God's relation to mankind. Persons of this sort tend to be extraordinarily self-centered, even though they may not be selfish in the usual sense of the word. Orual is a just ruler and capable of kindness to those about her. But for years she harbors a deep resentment because she has lost Psyche. In effect, Psyche has been unfaithful to her in preferring her god-husband to her sister.

It is the fanaticism of total attachment which comes close to destroying Orual. And with total attachment goes the unspoken demand for reciprocity. In the spiritual realm its fruit is the grief of the semidivine Psyche; in the temporal, the death of Orual's faithful captain, Bardia, consumed by his constant and uncomplaining devotion to his queen. In the poignant scene where Orual tries to console Bardia's wife, Ansit, only to be told that she has slowly used him up with her constant demands, we have a foretaste of the even more horrifying account of Orual's purgation for the sin against Psyche. To her, apparently, loving and devouring are the same. As Ansit says, "Perhaps you who spring from the gods love like the gods. Like the Shadowbrute, they say the loving and the devouring are all one, don't they?"[7] Yet Orual's love is not divine; it is all too human and earthly.

The concept of loving and devouring has its particular significance in the mixture of adoration and awe or even fear with which the Christian contemplates God. This idea plays a central part in the novel, from Psyche's union with the Shadowbrute to the terrifying scene of Orual's trial and judgment. The implications in loving and devouring go deep within the mystery of the godhead, though it is by no means another way of describing the wrathful God of the Old Testament. It is, for one thing, an aspect of sacramental experience. We both love God and symbolically devour him in the bread and wine of the Eucharist. More than that, it is a recognition of the awe-inspiring power of God, so great, so unmeasurable that it very often brings terror to those who contemplate and can in no way match it. In *Mere Christianity,* Lewis said that "God is the only comfort. He is also the supréme terror." Very often this terror comes to those who are overwhelmed by the violence and evil which God has allowed to exist in the world. The poet William Blake was harried by dark questionings as he tried to understand the meaning of a fierce jungle beast:

> Tyger, tyger, burning bright
> In the forests of the night,
> What immortal hand or eye
> Could frame thy fearful symmetry?

Often the consciousness of danger within the divine takes the form of an unresolved conflict between beauty and disaster, as in the conclusion of Coleridge's "Kubla Khan," in which the poet is to be exorcised by incantations because he has "drunk the milk of Paradise." The terror which God inspires arises from an awareness of the awful power which he can wield over men. Lewis paraphrases Denis de Rougemont in saying that love "begins to be a demon the moment he begins to be a god."[8] And he writes of love in terms that could be directly applied to Orual. "Every human love, at its height, has a tendency to claim for itself a divine authority. Its voice tends to sound as if it were the will of God himself. It tells us not to count the cost, it demands of us a total commitment, it attempts to override all other claims and insinuates that any action which is sincerely done 'for love's sake' is thereby lawful and even meritorious."[9] A possessive love is therefore an arrant example of the sin of presumption.

In his treatise *Four Loves,* Lewis defines agape as love in the Christian sense: God's love for humankind and the Christian's love for his fellows. This love, he says, is fraught with danger, for it involves the difficult transformation of one's natural love into a higher form. "To love at all," says Lewis, "is to be vulnerable. Love anything and your heart will certainly be wrung and possibly be broken."[10] Yet if natural love is to be changed into agape, there must be a kind of death. How painful this death can be is illustrated vividly in *Till We Have Faces*. The steps leading to this death are dangerous and terrible. When Orual finds Psyche on the mountain and hears her tale of her union with the god, she is in an agony of suspense. The girl must be mad, she thinks; she must be saved. She plunges a dagger into her arm and threatens suicide unless Psyche will consent to light a lamp and see her lover's face. And after the lamp is lit and she hears Psyche's voice in woeful lamentation fading away in the distance, her own sister banished from her newfound happiness, it is almost more than she can bear. Her whole life thereafter, until the redemption at the very end, seems, in Shakespeare's words, to be bound in shallows and miseries. She rules with a steely efficiency, locking away the passion of her love in a secret compartment, where it is hidden but never dies. This is the period of her life when she most clearly follows the teaching of her tutor, the Greek Lysias. In him, the disciple of Hellenic philosophy, the conduct of life is a rational exercise. The lucidity of logic is a solvent for the perplexities and the mysteries of experience. Orual turns to pragmatism in despair, to a kind of death of her best self.

In Psyche also there is a death. She is condemned to be a wanderer, separated from her god-lover. Yet there is probably more solace for her in this state than for Orual in hers. In the first place, she has become semidivine, and eventually a temple is raised in her honor. Years after Psyche's banishment, Orual comes upon this temple in a pleasant spot, and hears of the worshiped goddess, her sister. In another and far subtler way, however, Psyche is more fortunate than Orual. For, in a sense, the two sisters have been united. After Psyche looks upon her lover, a great voice says to Orual: "Now Psyche goes out in exile. Now she must hunger and thirst and tread hard roads. Those against whom I cannot fight must do their will upon her. You, woman, shall know yourself and your work. You also shall be

Psyche."[11] In other words, a psychological and spiritual relationship has been created whereby the sisters are indissolubly bound together. Orual, therefore, to put it in Christian terms, takes Psyche's sin upon herself, and vice versa. The dramatic possibilities of this doctrine were doubtless emphasized in Lewis's mind by their striking use in the poems and novels of his friend Charles Williams. Here the theory was known as "coinherence." Lewis explained it in his commentary on Williams' unfinished study of the Arthurian legend as a mutual interchange, a substitution or identification of one person for another.

[Such people] experience, above and beyond particular substitutions, that total reciprocity or co-inherence which first exists in the Blessed Trinity and descends thence into Man who was made in the image of the Trinity and is lost in Man by the Fall and restored to Man by "the one adored substitution" of Christ. What the Co-inherence means is best seen in the instance of the Blessed Virgin: Christ is born (and borne) of her: she is born (and borne) of Christ. So in humanity as a whole there is not merely an interchange of symmetrical relations (as when, A being the brother of B, B is also the brother of A) but of those unsymmetrical relations which seem incompatible on the level of "rational virtue." Each is mother and child, confessor and penitent, teacher and pupil, lord and slave to the other. Each is his neighbour's priest—and victim.[12]

Orual's identification with Psyche, however, entails years and years of suffering before the expiation of her sin. Before this occurs, there must come another kind of substitution for her, one that fills her with loathing. After her interview with Ansit, Bardia's wife (which probably constitutes the climax of the story), she begins to realize the disastrous results of her all-enveloping love. In the supernatural experience of her loss of Psyche, there has always remained resentment against something malicious and mysterious which she cannot explain; her condemnation by Ansit is clear and unanswerable. The shock is so great that she punishes herself in a way that seems peculiarly debasing: she gives up the veil which has kept her face hidden for so many years, flaunting her ugliness as a kind of penance. At that moment she realizes that *she* is the abominable goddess Ungit. A flicker of satisfaction comes to her when she realizes that if the people saw her, they would worship her as a holy person, but the feeling quickly passes. Her revulsion and despair begin the process of her purgation.

> To say that I was Ungit meant that I was as ugly in soul as she; greedy, blood-gorged. But if I practised true philosophy, as Socrates meant it, I should change my ugly soul into a fair one. And this, the gods helping me, I would do.[13]

So the philosophy of the Greeks, which once was somewhat cold comfort to her, adds its weight to her passionate despair and determination.

The resolution of Orual's difficulties comes with a final substitution of great poignancy and power. She finds herself in Psyche's presence in a series of visions. Ofter Psyche is laboring and poorly clothed, yet she does not appear to be suffering; in fact, she seems to be singing. "How can this be?" Orual asks the ghost of Lysias. He replies, "Another bore nearly all the anguish." Finally, the sisters find themselves in the presence of the god. As Orual looks into a pool, she discovers that she has been transformed into a radiant creature, into the likeness of Psyche. Orual's repentance, begun after her interview with Ansit, has been crowned not only with absolution but also with a new life of extraordinary beauty. Her death a short while later, in the serenity of her renewed and purified love for Psyche, is an act of gentle mercy.

One recognizes that there are two kinds of death in *Till We Have Faces*. There is the physical death of King Trom, a shabby end to a heavy, blustering father who gave his daughters little reason to love him, or the death of Prince Argan from the clean sword thrust in his duel with Orual, or the bodily death of Orual herself. The kind of death which is particularly meaningful in Lewis's novel, however, is not of this sort; it is symbolic, a figurative recognition of a spiritual rather than a physical end. It does not go so far in overt intention as Orual's threat to commit suicide if Psyche will not do as she says. It is instead a mysterious decision of numinous powers, whereby the person affected becomes aware of a profound transformation. This kind of death is Orual's problem from the time when, in her anguish over the disappearance of Psyche, she says to herself. "Orual dies if she ceases to love Psyche." Indeed, she does undergo a kind of "little death" during the long years when she reigns as queen, locking her remembrance of Psyche deep within herself, not daring to let it come to the surface of her conscious emotions. In the end, however, her symbolic death is a profound spiritual experience, and one with powerful Christian significance. In one of her purgative visions at the end of the novel, she sees herself (as indeed she had seen Psyche—another instance of substitution or coinherence) tying her ankles together at the edge of the river so that she cannot swim when she attempts to drown herself.

A voice came from beyond the river: "Do not do it." Instantly—I had been freezing cold till now—a wave of fire passed over me; even down to my numb feet. It was the voice of a god. Who should know better than I? A god's voice had once shattered my whole life. They are not to be mistaken. It may well be that, by trickery of priests, men have sometimes taken a mortal's voice for a god's. But it will not work the other way. No one who hears a god's voice takes it for a mortal's.

"Lord, who are you?" said I.

"Do not do it," said the god. "You cannot escape Ungit by going to the deadlands, for she is there also. Die before you die. There is no chance after."

The meaning of the god's words is quite clear. Orual is being told that she must die to sin; unless she does that, there is no hope for her after her physical death. This is the only road to absolution. Orual realizes the truth of the god's words. "The voice of the god," she says, "had not changed in all those years, but I had. There was no rebel in me now. I must not drown and doubtless should not be able to."[14]

It is Orual's problem rather than Psyche's which cries out for resolution. Though we know that Psyche goes through the world a sorrowing outcast after her banishment by the god, we never follow her and can only guess at her plight. More than that, however, we are not deeply involved in her unhappiness because of what she is. It will be remembered that Lewis, in his letter to Kilby, referred to her as *anima naturaliter christiana,* in other words, by her very nature a Christian soul, even though living in a pagan world. Indeed, Lewis says that in some ways she is Christ-like. This being so, there are the obvious parallels. First there is her beauty, not only of body but more especially of spirit.

As the Fox delighted to say, she was "according to nature"; what every woman, or even every thing, ought to have been and meant to be, but had missed by some trip of chance. Indeed, when you looked at her you believed, for a moment, that they had not missed it. When she trod on mud, the mud was beautiful; when she ran in the rain, the rain was silver. When she picked up a toad—she had the strangest and, I thought, unchanciest love for all manner of brutes—the toad became beautiful.[15]

Even before she becomes a goddess, she seems to move in an aura of divinity. Early in the story she is taunted by her half-sister Redival for allowing people of the town to bow down before her and adore her, as if they were worshiping a goddess. Lysias the Fox says of her, "Terribly does she resemble an undying spirit." And the priest of Ungit speaks darkly to the king of "terrible doings in this land; mortals aping the gods and stealing the worship due to the gods. . . ." The fearsome weight of holiness bears down upon her. There comes the day when she is despised and rejected by the townsfolk. She is called "accursed" because the people say she has made herself a goddess. Inevitably, the lot falls to her when the priest of Ungit seeks a sacrifice to appease the gods in the time of plague and drought. The Fox vainly argues against the choice of Psyche, asking why the best person in the land should also be the accursed. The priest answers in words of deep Christian significance: "Why should the Accursed not be both the best and the worst?" Psyche goes to her Mount, therefore, and is fastened to a tree, and comes to a new life.

The parellel to Christ is, of course, not complete. Psyche's "resurrection" entails years of wandering and suffering, yet in the end she is the instrument of redemption and salvation. She has Christ's compassion for suffering and sinful people, especially at the end for Orual's years of torment. And earlier, when she is about to leave for her sacrificial journey, she speaks familiar words. Orual suggests that Psyche send Redival her curse, since it was she who first babbled of her divinity to the priest of Ungit. But Psyche refuses, saying, "She also does what she doesn't know." As a natural Christian soul, forgiveness comes easily to her.

Psyche, for all her transparent goodness, seems like a perfectly real person, at least until her banishment by the god. After this she lives not in the natural world but in the supernatural, whence she returns, in a series of dreams or visions, to accomplish the redemption of Orual. She lives in the supernatural realm because she has an immense longing for otherworldly experience. This longing which is one of the most characteristic elements in Lewis's writings, this *Sehnsucht,* is a very powerful feeling compounded of yearning, melancholy, wonder, and an awareness of the numinous. Undoubtedly, his early passion for Germanic and Scandinavian legends, his "Northernness," helped to form this feeling. Later, after his reconversion to Christianity, it seemed to be an expression of a deep philosophical yearning for the fullness of Christian reward, a state of mind quite different from mystical exaltation, at times even suggesting the exhaustion of surrender after a hard conflict.

Perhaps this is the real meaning of his autobiographical account, *Surprised by Joy;* possibly he really was surprised by joy, surprised that joy could show so solemn a face. In any case, joy obviously had to be interpreted as something different from hedonism. In Lewis's case it can probably be described as a deep, awful wonder at the glory of God's power and love and at the dedication which leads the Christian to Him. For Lewis, Christianity was not a "comfortable" religion; as Orual realizes, "the Divine Nature wounds and perhaps destroys us merely by being what it is." But she also realizes that the gods love beauty of soul. For Lewis, this beauty of soul consists in surrender to God and in the reverent contemplation of eschatology—that is, death and resurrection. As Orual contemplates the horrible revelation that she is Ungit, she remembers a statement made by Socrates that "true wisdom is the skill and practice of death." Here, then, is a beginning, an end to passions, doubts, and perplexities, and entrance into a new life, a Heaven whose rewards are as unlike mundane rewards as can possibly be conceived.

Not without significance did Lewis entitle the last chapter of *Surprised by Joy* "The Beginning," an entering into the promise of life such as he had never known before. The choosing of God brings a kind of beauty to the least or the greatest of men; it made Orual as radiant as Psyche. This longing for the final access of grace, this desire for Heaven, is perhaps the strongest element in Lewis's religious faith. He reveals it vividly and dramatically in his novel *The Great Divorce*, in which a group of persons from the great gray city of Hell, where people cannot communicate with each other, are taken to Heaven as a test of their ability or willingness to stay. Only one of the pilgrims qualifies; death has not taught the others the true meaning of Heaven. They are still confined in worldly aims and prejudices. The author George Macdonald, one of the heavenly host, says to the narrator: "Love, as mortals understand the word, isn't enough. Every natural love will rise again and live forever in this country: but none will rise again until it has been buried";[16] in other words, until it has been transformed and purified by death. It is a shattering picture that Lewis draws in *The Great Divorce*, of men completely blind to the unimaginable joys of paradise, as shattering as the "Un-Man" Weston's attempt in *Perelandra* to re-enact the fall of Man in a new garden of Eden. It is the consciousness of what man rejects, the rewards he might have if only he would stretch out his hand for them, that lies at the heart of Lewis's *Sehnsucht*.

Till We Have Faces is the most concentrated and the most powerful expression of Lewis's religious belief to be found in any of his novels. Whereas in the planetary trilogy, Lewis was concerned with the fate of mankind under the danger of attack by sinister "Macrobes" from outer space, in *Till We Have Faces* our attention is directed to the fate of two women. Though the story makes frequent and effective use of supernatural elements found in the myth of Cupid and Psyche, the emphasis is not upon legendary wonders, but rather on subtle and complicated issues raised by the estrangement of Orual and her sister. The novel develops through philosophical and theological crises which, in spite of a setting in a pagan, pre-Christian land, have very strong correspondences with Christian belief. In fact, it is not too much to say that it constitutes one of the most powerful of Lewis's religious works, filled with intense fervor and deep conviction, expressed for the most part in a manner markedly different from that of the planetary trilogy, a style almost classical in its directness, simplicity, and logical force; yet also capable of rising, in moments of wonder either supernatural or philosophical, to true eloquence. Lewis's friend Owen Barfield said that, in his opinion, *Till We Have Faces* was "the most muscular and powerful product of Lewis's imagination."[17] John Lawlor, a former student of Lewis's, wrote with perceptive insight: "There is one other piece of narrative to be mentioned, and I would place it above all others. *Till We Have Faces* is truly a 'myth' in the sense which Lewis himself defined in his *Experiment in Criticism*—a story which 'depends hardly at all on such usual narrative attractions as suspense or surprise' and communicates the sense of that which is 'not only grave but awe-inspiring.' For once, Lewis attained something which he approved above all else and for which he revered Camus, a 'dearly bought singleness of quality—Smooth and full as if one gush/ Of life had washed it!' "[18]

There is indeed a singleness of quality in *Till We Have Faces*, especially in its grave concentration upon the alienation and reconciliation of two women who live both in the real and in the supernatural world. Notice that the word is singular, "world," rather than "worlds." Like his great friend Charles Williams, Lewis found it difficult if not impossible to differentiate between the two. In *Miracles* he says, "The supernatural is not remote and abstruse: it is a matter of daily and hourly experience, as intimate as breathing." In *The Weight of Glory* he speaks of the transcending wonder of human beings. "The load, or weight, or burden of my neighbour's glory should be laid daily on my back, a load so heavy that only humility can carry it, and the backs of the proud will be broken. It is a serious thing to live in a society of possible gods and goddesses. . . . There are no ordinary people. You have never talked to a mere mortal. . . . It is immortals whom we joke with, work with, marry, snub and exploit —immortal horrors or everlasting splendours."[19]

Over and over again, whether in his fiction or in his other prose, Lewis gives us a vision of a world not made with hands, and of people infused with grace who struggle upward toward Heaven, much as the fourteenth-century Walter Hylton, in *The Ladder of Perfection*, likened the progress of the soul to a pilgrimage to Jerusalem: "Jerusalem is as moche as to saye as a syght of peace, and betokeneth contemplacyon in parfyte love of God."

Finally, Lewis gives us an acute awareness of the contemporaneity of all human experience. *Till We Have Faces* is no exercise in archaism, no period piece tricked out in fancy dress. It is triumphantly a tract for the times. It makes the wisdom of ancient peoples relevant to conduct in the twentieth century; as Lewis said, in speaking of fantastic stories, instead of commenting on life, they can add to it. On these terms the pagan love and forbearance of Psyche are indistinguishable from Christian virtues; the rational axioms of Lysias the Fox, the moral insights of Socrates (a Christian before Christ), are as valid guides to conduct as ever they were two or more millennia ago. Stella Gibbons speaks pertinently to this point: "It has been suggested to me that in *Till We Have Faces* Lewis saw one of what he called 'good dreams' or 'those queer stories scattered all throughout heathen religions'; pre-Christian hints of the Christian relationship between Adam and his Creator."[20] Lewis's habit of mind was centrifugal; his expanding comprehension inevitably regarded past and present as inseparable. Each was immediate, each was dynamic. Henry David Thoreau's statement, in *Walden*, that "Olympus is but the outside of the earth everywhere" would have delighted him. Ancient Greece sheds her glory on the earth over which we move every day. He would have delighted also in Thoreau's belief that "Heaven is under our feet as well as over our heads." Body and spirit are one; the physical being we call man cannot escape the mysteries of divine visitation. Seldom has this visitation been described with more subtlety and power than in *Till We Have Faces*. Lewis is rightly one of a great and honorable company.

Notes

1. *Letters of C. S. Lewis* (to Fr. Peter Milward), ed. W. H. Lewis (London: Geoffrey Bles, 1966), p. 271.
2. C. S. Lewis, *Of Other Worlds* (New York: Harcourt, Brace & World, 1967), p. 88.
3. *Ibid.*, p. 38.
4. *The Allegory of Love* (London and New York: Oxford University Press, 1948), p. 83.
5. *Letters*, pp. 273-74.
6. *The Four Loves* (New York: Harcourt, Brace & World, 1960), p. 19.
7. *Till We Have Faces* (London: Geoffrey Bles, 1956), p. 275.
8. *The Four Loves*, p. 17.
9. *Ibid.*, p. 17.
10. *Ibid.*, p. 166.
11. *Till We Have Faces*, p. 182.
12. Charles Williams, *Arthurian Torso* (London and New York: Oxford University Press, 1948), p. 143.
13. *Till We Have Faces*, pp. 292-93.
14. *Ibid.*, pp. 290-91.
15. *Ibid.*, pp. 30-31.
16. *The Great Divorce* (New York: The Macmillan Company, 1946), p. 98.
17. *Light on C. S. Lewis*, ed. Jocelyn Gibb (London: Geoffrey Bles, 1965), p. xx.
18. *Ibid.*, p. 81.
19. *The Weight of Glory* (New York: The Macmillan Company, 1949), pp. 14-15.
20. *Light on C. S. Lewis*, p. 94.

The Plague

An Introduction and Commentary

The Plague is a modern myth about the destiny of man. Speaking as an artist rather than as a professional philosopher, Camus comes to grips with the problems of evil and unhappiness, not only on the level of the individual person and of society but also in their metaphysical dimension. He directly confronts the ancient problem which Christianity discusses in terms of original sin, actual sin, suffering, and redemption. Like traditional Christianity, Camus solves the problem in terms of human freedom; but where Christianity introduces a higher dimension of liberty, the gift of divine freedom which is called grace, Camus finds the concept of grace impossible to accept. Is that perhaps because he has been deceived by the distorted notion of grace which some Christians find amply sufficient? The present commentary will pay particular attention to this problem. But meanwhile, the novel must be read not simply as a drama or as a psychological study, but as a myth of good and evil, of freedom and historical determinism, of love against what Hopkins called "the death dance in our blood."

For Camus, this "death dance," this hidden propensity to pestilence, is something more than mere mortality. It is the willful negation of life that is built into life itself: the human instinct to dominate and to destroy—to seek one's own happiness by destroying the happiness of others, to build one's security on power and, by extension, to justify evil use of that power in terms of "history," or of "the common good," or of "the revolution," or even of "the justice of God."

Man's drive to destroy, to kill, or simply to dominate and to oppress comes from the metaphysical void he experiences when he finds himself a stranger in his own universe. He seeks to make that universe familiar to himself by using it for his own ends, but his own ends are capricious and ambivalent. They may be life-affirming, they may be expressions of comprehension and of love, or they may be life-denying, armored in legalism and false theology, or perhaps even speaking the naked language of brute power. In any case, the message of Camus is that man cannot successfully seek the explanation of his existence in abstractions: instead of trying to justify his life in terms of abstract formulas, man must create meaning in his existence by living in a meaningful way. In the words of Maurice Cranston, for Camus "the world has no ultimate meaning . . . but something in it has meaning . . . man, the only creature to insist on having one."[1]

The Plague affirms this clearly. The frightful visitation of pestilence is met with men's insistence on retaining their meaning. The book is a protest against all forms of passive submission to unhappiness and unmeaning. It is a protest against the passive acceptance of alienation. This protest is explicitly nonreligious. Camus even called The Plague "the most anti-Christian" of his books. Yet Camus was at once too honest and too modest to be rigidly doctrinaire in his attitude toward religion. He was not an atheist, still less a militant atheist. He simply confessed that the Christian experience was something entirely foreign to his life and that he therefore could not really identify himself with Christians. His treatment of Christianity is ironic and severe, but not totally without sympathy. It is typical of the "post-Christian" mentality which bases its criticism of Christianity on the historic gap between a glorious Christian ideal and a somewhat less edifying reality. There are elements in Camus himself which suggest that Christian grace and liberty may perhaps have contributed unconsciously to the formation of his own austere and compassionate ethic.

Camus is sometimes represented as having preached "the absurd." Nothing could be more mistaken. He wants his reader to recognize "the absurd" in order to resist it. "The absurd" is simply one face of "the Plague" which we must resist in all its aspects. The Plague is the tyranny of evil and of death, no matter what form it may take: the Nazi occupation of France, the death camps, the bourgeois hypocrisy of the French system (which Camus had observed in action in Algeria), Stalinism, or the unprincipled opportunism of certain French Marxists. All such types uneasily sensed that The Plague was talking about them—and we might add that the same Plague is not absent from the United States today.

One thing must be made quite clear. Camus is resolutely opposed to a facile historicism which, in the name of "progress" and of the "future," exploits and sacrifices living man here and now. In an interview in New York in 1946, Camus said: "If the problem of mankind boils down to an historical task, whatever that task may be, man is no longer anything but the raw material of history, and one can do with him what one wishes." The presence in our world of a cynical, unprincipled appetite for power which seeks to "do with man what one wishes" is what Camus has symbolized, in this myth-novel, by the hideous figure of the Plague. If Camus is severe with Christians, it is because he thinks they have abdicated their mission of opposing the Plague and have instead devoted their talents to excusing and justifying it in terms of an ambiguous theology or (as in his story *The Renegade*) by compromise with political absolutism.

About the Author

Though he fully identified himself with Algeria, where he was born in 1913 and grew up among working-class people of European extraction, Camus could not really be considered a voice of the "Third World." On the other hand, he could not be called a spokesman for France or for Europe, where he always felt himself to be to some extent a stranger and an exile. Actually, Camus is a cosmopolitan twentieth-century man born in Africa and familiar with Europe, South America, and the United States. Citizen of a colony which, during his lifetime, took up arms to free itself from a European mother country, he lost his father in World War I (in the battle of the Marne). Rejected by the armed forces because he was tubercular, he nevertheless took an active part in the French resistance to Nazism in World War II. Though he was, like many others in the thirties, drawn to Communism, he later repudiated Stalinist power politics and remained aloof from Marxism, which he thought to be basically antihumanist. On the other hand, he did not, like so many other ex-Marxists, go over to the right wing, but maintained a precariously conscientious and personal attitude which was critical of all doctrinaire positions and earned him a great deal of obloquy from all sides.

Camus grew up in the care of his mother, a Spaniard who had given up all practice of her Catholic faith. He adopted her attitude of quiet contempt for the religiosity of old people in the neighborhood, especially his own devout grandmother, considering their religion simply an evasion of life and an attempt to find justification for an existence that drifted helplessly toward death. His first book of essays and sketches, *L'envers et l'endroit* (1937), ironically observed the religion of the old and preferred the frank, skeptical, life-loving paganism of the Algerian youth on the sunny Mediterranean beaches. The sun, the sea, the shore, the Algerian countryside dotted with half-hidden Roman ruins—all spoke to Camus of what he most valued: the life-affirming heritage of Mediterranean culture, particularly Greek culture. But he was also alert to the ambiguities of the Greek tradition, sensitive to the tragic view of life that was born of the Athenian theater and to the dualistic spirituality of Neoplatonism.

At the University of Algiers, Camus wrote a thesis (1936) on early Christianity, Neoplatonism, Gnosticism, and St. Augustine. He attempted to explain the Augustinian attitude toward evil, which he found deeply repugnant, by the influence of Manichaeism and Neoplatonism. This theme still concerned him in *The Plague*, where the Augustinian preoccupation with physical evil as the punishment of sin obsesses the Jesuit Père Paneloux.

During his university studies Camus contracted an unsuccessful civil marriage, which broke up in 1935. Meanwhile, he joined the Communist party and worked among the oppressed Moslems. His most productive work after leaving the university was in the theater, where he wrote and produced plays, with strong political implications, for a cast of working-class actors. After leaving the Communists in 1937, he joined the Algerian Movement of National Liberation and, working for a left-wing paper, did a highly competent series of articles on the famine in Kabylia. When his paper was suppressed by the government in 1940, Camus went to France, which was by this time at war. Unable to enlist because of his health, Camus continued his newspaper work in Paris and finished his first novel, *The Stranger*, published in 1942. A second marriage, a series of physical breakdowns, trips to and from North Africa, periods of convalescence and rest in central France, publication of the philosophical essay *The Myth of Sisyphus*, work on his first plays, participation in the French Resistance—all this occupied Camus during the war years, and out of this activity came *The Plague*, which certainly, on one level at least, reflects the tension, the fatigue, the struggle, the sense of frustration and dogged rebellion which dominated France under the Nazis.

Camus lived and taught school in Oran, the scene of *The Plague*, for a brief period in 1941. During that time there was a typhoid epidemic in the city. The first notes for *The Plague* were written in April 1941.

The liberating plague

Happy town. People live according to different systems. The plague: abolishes all systems. But they are all the same.

Doubly useless . . .[2]

Elsewhere he reflects that people are always ready to write books on Florence or Athens—but who would write of a place like Oran? "No one would have the idea of writing about a town where there is nothing to attract the mind, where ugliness has played an overwhelming role and where the past is reduced to nothing."[3]

He was already tempted to write about Oran, for if the town was ugly and boring, there was nevertheless something to write about. "My reply is: human beings."

When it appeared in 1947, *The Plague* was an instant success. Everyone recognized the experience of the war years as well as a deeper, more universal question about the meaning of life itself in the contemporary world. The war had shown Camus—and everyone else—that the placid surface of routine and prosperous middle-class existence opened out into a metaphysical and moral abyss that was both incomprehensible and frightening. Though Camus was no philosopher and no existentialist, his first two novels displayed all the irony, the austerity, the bizarre, laconic, and ruthlessly critical analysis of man and society which readers expected from Sartre.

Thus far, Sartre and Camus were friends, though there were always obvious and significant differences between them. In 1952, however, after Camus' essay on revolution, *L'homme revolté*, the two authors broke with one another and became embroiled in one of those interminable, acid controversies which seem so necessary in the intellectual world, particularly in Paris.

In May, 1956, Camus published his third and last novel, *The Fall*. Thereafter he devoted his time and energy to work in the theater, writing and producing plays based on Faulkner (*Requiem for a Nun*, 1956) and Dostoievski (*The Possessed*, 1959). Meanwhile, he was awarded the Nobel Prize for literature in 1957, when he was still in his forties. Camus never reached the age of fifty. On January 4, 1960, while driving from southern France to Paris with his publisher, he was killed in an accident.

The work of a brilliant French writer—one of the best of his time —was thus cut off at the peak of his development. We know from his *Notebooks* (which have since been published) that he had other and perhaps more important work in progress. We know that having started with the problem of "the absurd" in his first novel and in *Sisyphus,* he had gone on to develop the ethic of revolt— above all in *The Plague. The Fall,* brilliant though it may be, represents a dead end, a *ne plus ultra* in futile self-examination. Clamence, the penitent-judge, is the reduction to the absurd of all that Camus has to say about the sterility of a society that is built, as Tarrou in *The Plague* observes, on institutions whose chief aim seems to be to justify evil, injustice, and death.

Perhaps *The Fall* belonged to what the *Notebooks* call "the cycle of Nemesis," which would also have included a book on the Nazi death camps. Finally, however, Camus was planning to deal with what most attracted him: a "certain kind of love"—a fuller development of those life-affirming themes which we find in some of his early essays and also in the conversations between Rieux and Tarrou in *The Plague.* Camus never had a chance to develop further the austere, almost stoic idealism of the "healer" who fights against disease and death because living man remains for him an ultimate, inexplicable value. He never more fully explored the mysterious and controversial heroism of "the saint without God" that Tarrou wanted to be—and that Camus himself could never quite accept. But Camus was always attracted to the cryptic idealism of Tarrou, just as he had been to the quasi-mystical spirituality of Plotinus.

In the end, Camus' deepest affirmation is that of an almost traditional and classic humanism, with a few significant modern doubts, austerities, and reservations. Camus is definitely not an existentialist. He rests his work on basic assumptions about the nature of man, even though he never spells out these assumptions in clearly essentialist terms. The work of Camus is a humanism rooted in man as authentic value; in life, which is to be affirmed in defiance of suffering and death; in love, compassion, and understanding, the solidarity of men in revolt against the absurd, men whose comradeship has a certain purity because it is based on the renunciation of all illusions, all misleading ideals, all deceptive and hypocritical social forms.

What Camus really wanted to explore was the possibility of a new and authentic humanism based not on religious or political ideologies, to which the individual may all too easily be sacrificed, but on a deeply authentic relationship between living human persons. In the words of his Nobel Prize acceptance speech, Camus wanted to show men how to "fashion an art of living in times of catastrophe, to be reborn by fighting openly against the death instinct at work in our society." Nowhere in all his work did he achieve this aim more convincingly than in *The Plague*.

Introduction to the Book

A typical French colonial city—banal, placid, engrossed in its business and in its routine pleasures, a little city without ideas, a community without character, where nothing special is supposed to happen—is suddenly struck by a disease which has vanished from the civilized world: bubonic plague. Oran, Algeria (described elsewhere by Camus as a labyrinth where the wanderer is destroyed by the Minotaur of boredom), is presented as typically "modern." Not, of course, that it is frantically progressive, or that it moves particularly fast, or that it sees far ahead. Yet it is modern in the sense that it "has no past." Modern, too, in the sense that it is populated entirely by enlightened humanists who do not believe in bubonic plague.

The measure of Oran is the measure of modern man in his banality, his love of system, his routine practicality, his indifference to life in depth, whether in sorrow or in joy. The Oranais shares a universal modern conviction that the action is taking place somewhere else. Well, for once, the action takes place in Oran. In fact, the city, visited by pestilence, is entirely cut off from the outside world for ten months. Oran becomes a hectic and beleaguered little world in which the struggle for existence is a bizarre and incredibly difficult affair. A large proportion of the population is killed off. That their town should have "been chosen out for the scene of such grotesque happenings" is, for the Oranais, a rude and salutary shock. It inspires reflection, at least for a while. And then life itself becomes so exacting that one can hardly think; but all, in one way or other, come to realize that the fight against the Plague is everybody's concern. Some dedicate themselves completely to the work of keeping the Plague in check, saving lives, caring for the sick, burying the dead. Many lay down their own lives, not as "heroes" but simply because it is what they have to do.

It was said above that Oran is "typical." The citizens are supposed to be the most ordinary kind of people: modern middle- and working-class Frenchmen living in Algeria. But Oran is not a typical *Algerian* city. Nowhere in the book does an Arab appear. The characters are all Europeans or of European descent. This is perhaps significant. The Plague described by Camus is a plague for *Europeans*—who happen in this case also to be "colonialists." That is why he chose Oran instead of Algiers or Constantine as the scene of his story. Oran is a new city, a completely French city with no *Kasbah*. The fact that the people in the book are for the most part French—there are one or two Spaniards—reminds us that the book, on one of its levels, is also a story of the Nazi occupation in France. The Plague is not only the physical epidemic but also the moral sickness of men under oppression by a hateful regime— a typological reign of evil.

We observe the plague-stricken city through the eyes of a detached, coolly objective witness who speaks in matter-of-fact tones, avoiding all drama and all overstatement, and yet with an authentic personal involvement in the struggle to save lives. Sometimes he draws on the notebook of another witness, Tarrou, a man of ironic and compassionate humor who turns out to be a kind of "saint without God"—or at least who aspires to that condition. Tarrou's notes, as quoted by the narrator, may also be found in the *Notebooks*, but we cannot say that Camus identifies himself with Tarrou. The central character of the book is Dr. Rieux, who is one of the first to identify the Plague and one of the few who, in spite of his constant daily contact with the victims, comes through unharmed.

The narrative begins when Dr. Rieux finds a dead rat on the landing outside his apartment. Within a few days, scores and then hundreds of dead rats show up everywhere. Soon humans begin to fall ill and die. Dr. Rieux diagnoses bubonic plague, but has a difficult time getting the city officials to admit the facts and take the necessary measures. Finally the city is closed off, and since it is surrounded by fortifications, this is not difficult. All contact with the outside world, except by telephone, telegraph, and radio, comes to an end. There is no plague serum on hand. The supply ordered from Paris is a long time coming and proves ineffective. The sickness takes hold of the population. All available public buildings are turned into hospitals. Quarantine camps are set up in various places—for instance, in the municipal stadium; food grows scarce; a black market flourishes. However, the cafes continue to be well frequented, and so do the movie houses, in spite of the fact that the same pictures have to be shown over and over again.

Meanwhile, religion offers an answer to the tragic problem of pestilence. Père Paneloux, a prominent local Jesuit with a reputation for solid scholarship as well as for militant Christianity, preaches a sermon on the Plague. The sermon contains "vigorous home truths." Oran has the Plague because this is what the people deserve. God is disappointed with the modern world in general and with them in particular. But in his mercy God is giving the city another chance. The Plague is a summons to awaken from religious indifference. Perhaps this is a seed time for a future harvest. Perhaps the Plague lights the path to future salvation. With St. Augustine, whom Paneloux acknowledges as his master, he believes the Plague "reveals the will of God in action unfailingly transforming evil into good." The theme of the Plague as punishment for sin echoes the preaching of many French Catholic priests and bishops after the fall of France during "the great penitence of Vichy."

Meanwhile, a journalist, Rambert, is working on an elaborate plan to escape from the city and rejoin his young wife in France. In contrast, Tarrou organizes volunteer sanitation squads, under the immediate direction of Rieux, whose members risk their lives in order to fight the Plague. A great deal of suspense is created by the fact that when Rambert's plan for escape has, after repeated difficulties, finally reached the point of probable success, he renounces it and joins Tarrou.

The Plague drags on, the men who fight it growing more and more exhausted. One of the doctors develops a serum taken from the victims themselves and tests it on a child, who dies in horrible suffering. But the unusual suffering of the child is due to the fact that the serum gave him power to fight the disease. Eventually the serum does prove effective. Meanwhile, the suffering and death of the child, in the presence of Paneloux and Rieux, once again brings up the problem of evil. Challenged by Rieux to justify the death of the innocent in religious terms, the Jesuit revises his previous declarations. He admits that his first sermon was "uncharitable," and instead of promulgating easy and definitive answers, confesses that he does not claim to "understand" the mystery of evil but nevertheless continues to "love what he cannot understand." His conclusion is no longer expressed in terms of judgment and punishment, but of self-abandonment and sacrifice. And, in fact, Paneloux also lays down his life in the struggle against the Plague, as a member of a sanitary squad. It is clear that the "sanitary squads" are meant to suggest the French Resistance units; and Paneloux's change of heart—he ends up fighting on the side of Rieux and Tarrou—represents the part played by some of the French Catholic clergy in the resistance against Nazism.

Finally the new serum begins to work. Patients who seemed hopelessly condemned, suddenly recover. The Plague is obviously beaten, but just as victory becomes certain, Tarrou catches the Plague and dies.

The last pages of the book describe the opening of the city gates, the coming of the first train, the reunion of Rambert with his wife, and the death of a black marketeer, Cottard, who suggests the French collaborationists. Amid the general celebration, Rieux walks the streets alone, reflecting on the struggle and its meaning, deciding "that there are more things to admire in man than to despise," but also thinking that the joy of the crowds is perhaps not as secure as they imagine: "the plague bacillus never dies or disappears for good . . . it can lie dormant . . . perhaps the day would come when, for the bane and the enlightening of men, it would rouse up its rats again and send them forth to die in a happy city."

In spite of these final words, *The Plague* remains the most positive and conclusive of all Camus' novels. The real drama of the book is found in the contrapuntal treatment of the theme of evil on two levels: the Plague as physical evil and the Plague as a deficiency in the human spirit, a challenge which summons up the deepest resources of the human conscience in its capacity for courage and love.

Discussion of Themes and Characters

The Face of the Plague. "They fancied themselves free," says Rieux of the Oranais, "and no one will ever be free as long as there are pestilences." And "there have been as many plagues as wars in history; yet always plagues and wars take people equally by surprise."

In one of Camus' plays, *The State of Siege*, the Plague appears as a totalitarian dictator. In this novel, the Plague is in a way the central character, though it remains faceless and impersonal. The Plague acts as though it has an arbitrary mind and will of its own. Breaking through the placid surface of everyday routine existence, it rudely imposes upon the citizens the dreadful facts of suffering, isolation, and sudden death. The Oranais are not prepared to believe in the Plague because it is not made to their measure. The Plague teaches them that there are certain things which are not made to man's measure, and not exactly to his liking, which he must nevertheless confront as fundamental realities of human existence.

A pestilence isn't a thing made to man's measure; therefore we tell ourselves that pestilence is a mere bogey of the mind, a bad dream that will pass away. But it doesn't always pass away, and, from one bad dream to another, it is men who pass away, and the humanists first of all, because they haven't taken their precautions. Our townsfolk were not more to blame than others; they forgot to be modest, that was all, and thought that everything still was possible for them, which presupposed that pestilences were impossible. They went on doing business, arranged for journeys, and formed views. How should they have given thought to anything like plague, which rules out any future, cancels journeys, silences the exchange of views?[4]

Plague here represents all the forms of evil which break in upon human existence and curtail the freedom of man by destroying the basic assumptions upon which he builds his plans for future action. Thinking which does not adequately account for evil cannot be called realistic. Freedom that presupposes such unreal thinking is not free. Camus summons the Plague to bear witness to the fact that no systematic thinking can be fully realistic if it excludes the radical *absurdity* of an existence into which evil or irrationality can always break without warning. Yet we seem to assume that human affairs can be laid out neatly in reasonable patterns, as if everything were always in order and as if this order were completely accessible to any mind that carefully studied causes and their effects. Dr. Rieux, by all odds the most objective and scientific mind in the book—the most authentic humanist—is also the one who comes closest to "knowing" the Plague. He is apparently the only one who is able to situate this epidemic in a historical context of bizarre and unpredictable disasters. He is aware that the clanging bells of the Oran trolley cars, which proceed to the cemeteries loaded with bodies, belong in a long procession with the death carts of London and Marseilles and draw our gaze back to the beaches of Attica, where the Athenians kindled huge pyres and fought fiercely with torches in order to throw their dead into the flames rather than into the sea.

"They forgot to be modest, that was all." *Modesty* is a key word in this book. It is an understatement, chosen half in irony. What is it? The sanity of that realistic self-assessment which delivers men from fatal *hubris*. The citizens of Oran were unaware of the miasma of evil which a keener moral sense would have quickly detected. The self-assurance of those who know all the answers in advance and who are convinced of their own absolute and infallible correctness, sets the stage for war, pestilence, famine, and other personages we prefer to leave unnoticed in the pages of an apocalypse. *Modesty,* in the vocabulary of Tarrou's notebook and of Camus himself, implies a capacity to doubt one's own wisdom, a hesitancy in the presence of doctrines and systems that explain everything too conveniently and justify evil as a kind of good. In Camus, this modesty is a lesson taught in the school of the absurd. It therefore has metaphysical—or antimetaphysical—resonances. The modesty of Tarrou and Rieux is antimetaphysical in the sense that it refuses to adorn with big words a mystery of being which it admits it cannot penetrate. But it is also metaphysical, at least in a sense acceptable to Gabriel Marcel, because it respects the more or less impenetrable truth, the baffling presence of the limitations imposed on man's existence as though by an arbitrary power. It is fully aware of the reality both of man's being and of his inexorable limits. It experiences at once the nobility and the poverty of man's freedom. It refuses to substitute grandiose and heroic ideals for the reality— the *modest* reality—of what man is actually capable of doing.

We find Rieux musing about the seriousness of the Plague which has just been discovered. Will the Plague die out just because it has been identified and resisted? Are lucidity and care and patience all that are needed? "He pulled himself together" (at the point where he was tempted to spell it out in a message of hope), hearing the sound of a man at work with a machine saw. "There lay certitude; there in the daily round. All the rest hung on mere threads and trivial contingencies; you couldn't waste your time on it. The thing was to do your job as it should be done."5

The Modest Certitudes. What is the difference between Rieux and the other people of Oran who also do their job each day, more or less as it should be done? His lucidity. They imagine that their everyday existence *proves something.* Indeed, they are satisfied with the thought that they themselves prove something, if not everything. They are engrossed in lives which they imagine to be, if not actually significant (because, after all, they may be bored, frustrated, secretly confused, or disillusioned), at least potentially so. They are convinced that there is a clear and simple meaning which is quite conclusive, which is the answer, the right answer, and that it is somehow embodied in an order to which they themselves bear witness insofar as they are happy, prosperous, comfortable, secure. They may not know that answer, or if they think they have dimly grasped it, they may not be able to formulate it. Never mind, they will delegate that responsibility to specialists. There are the officials of the city. They know the law. They represent the order which reflects a basic immutable truth. Or, if you happen to be a believer (a few of them have their moments of belief, which rarely last) there are theologians like Père Paneloux. And then there are doctors. And beyond all these there are still higher powers: higher governing officials, higher church dignitaries, and, in Paris, super-doctors who will send a serum to save everyone from the Plague. Unfortunately, the serum arrives late and proves ineffective.

The Plague breaks in upon all these people as a visitation of cosmic irony and tragedy. Suddenly their existence, their reasonable answers, their established order, their official clichés, are seen to be absurd. Dr. Rieux and his friend Tarrou are among the few who are able to defend themselves, in such a position, precisely because they have no desire *to prove anything*. They are willing to do their job, do it well, and even lay down their lives, *without insisting that anything is proved by their action*. In other words, without declaring that they are *justified* in doing what they do. The word "justified" is used here in a strong, quasi-theological sense—as if their action proved them to be in harmony with some Absolute Power.

Such is the modesty of Camus, refusing justification both by works and by faith. It is the modesty which simply elects to fight against death because life is a value beyond question. A modesty which also at the same time refuses to watch itself performing "praiseworthy acts" or "doing good" or even "being heroic." It refuses to preach about its acts, as if to imply "these are the acts everyone should perform." For example, Rieux refuses to argue that Rambert ought not to escape. He does not try to persuade Rambert to stay and fight the Plague with him. On the contrary, he admits that human love—for which Rambert wants to save his own life—is also something of an absolute, or at any rate a primary, value.

Rieux has standards which he has chosen for himself, but he hesitates to impose them on anyone else. When Tarrou offers to form "sanitary squads" and risk his life fighting the Plague, his motives are "modest" and he finds them almost laughable. They seem to imply that he has a code of morals, but he cannot quite define what that code is. Finally he tries to dismiss it in one admittedly inadequate word: "comprehension." This, too, one can guess, is going to turn out to be another key word in this book. Camus' key words are usually unexpected, chosen perhaps for a kind of obliquity which glances off the nail instead of pretending to hit it on the head. Another form of modesty! Only people like Judge Othon and Père Paneloux claim to hit nails squarely on the head. And they, too, must learn a more modest vocabulary from the Plague!

Perhaps one reason for this Camusian modesty and its distrust of formal virtuousness is that Camus is suspicious of success. Not that he entertains a superstitious fear of it, but he is repelled by an ethic of material success as the implicit reward for virtuousness—one of the more complacent myths of bourgeois society. It is ironic that *The Plague* was a great success, and won the French Critics' Prize for 1947. Camus then reacted in his *Notebooks*:

Melancholy of success. Opposition is essential. If everything were harder for me, as it was before, I should have much more right to say what I am saying. The fact remains that I can help many people—in the meantime.[6]

Camus was obviously aware of the fact that his critique of French society and of its criteria for success became ambiguous when that same society gave him the highest praise it could give a moralist, precisely because he distrusted virtue.

In the same notes, and in a rather subtle analysis, Camus tries to come to grips with this ambiguity. "Distrust of formal virtue—there is the explanation of this world." The Marxists, he reasons, proceed from this to call everything impure except what contributes to the Marxist cause: that becomes "virtue." But the conviction that "nothing is pure" has, Camus says, "poisoned our century." He admits that "everything I have ever thought or written is related to that distrust [it is the subject of *The Stranger*]." But even more than formal virtue, he distrusts the nihilism that negates all virtue in order to dedicate itself to revolutionary action in history, regardless of whether it is "moral" or not. Of the Marxists and the Sartrian ethic he says, "There are some who take up falsehood as one takes up a religious life." Camus tries to solve this problem in *L'homme revolté*: Can one engage validly in historical action without, on the one hand, indulging in the narcissism of "the virtuous conscience" and without, on the other, being a nihilist and ignoring all good and evil? His solution is sketched out in *The Plague*, and in the end the followers of Sartre would condemn Camus as a "pure soul."

At any rate, the modest narrator in *The Plague* refuses to praise the members of the sanitary squads as if they were heroes. He will not give them "more importance than is their due. . . ." The narrator is inclined to think that by attributing overimportance to praiseworthy actions one may by implication be paying indirect but potent homage to the worse side of human nature. "For this attitude implies that such actions shine out as rare exceptions . . . ."

The modesty of Rieux and Tarrou is based, therefore, on a fundamentally *optimistic* view of human nature, while the idealism it rejects may perhaps often conceal an actual pessimism in regard to human reality. What is "good" about the activity of Tarrou is not precisely the courage, which many others share, but the *comprehension* which sees and loves the goodness of his fellow man and subordinates that value to everything else.

Ignorance, the lack of comprehension, becomes an incorrigible vice and a great source of evil when it turns to dogmatism, "fancies it knows everything and therefore claims for itself the right to kill." The modesty and comprehension of Camus are, then, based not only on a realistic sense of the absurd but also on a deeply compassionate respect for life and for the concrete human person. The ignorance which Camus rejects ignores the absurd, and fancying itself to be wisdom, prefers its own rightness to the values that are worth defending. Indeed, it sacrifices those values by its willingness to kill men in honor of its dogmatic self-idolatry.

Camusian modesty and comprehension are, therefore, antiheroic. They speak in sober understatements, in quiet irony. They remain cool. Camus is not Promethean. His revolt is not that of the Titan who stormed heaven to steal fire from the gods, but of Sisyphus, the hero of the absurd (that is to say, the non-hero), who simply pushes a rock again and again to the top of a hill, and starts all over again each time the rock rolls back to the bottom. The work of Rieux and Tarrou against the Plague is just as dogged, in many ways just as absurd, as that of Sisyphus. There are moments when their exhausting and dangerous struggle seems utterly hopeless; but they continue anyway, not in order to prove themselves better than the Plague but simply because they are alive and they want to help others to stay alive.

Those who enrolled in the "sanitary squads" . . . had indeed, no such great merit in doing as they did, since they knew it was the only thing to do, and the unthinkable thing would then have been not to have brought themselves to do it. These groups enabled our townsfolk to come to grips with the disease and convinced them that now that the plague was among us, it was up to them to do whatever could be done to fight it. Since plague became in this way some men's duty, it revealed itself as what it really was: that is the concern of all.[7]

The narrator goes on to say that one does not praise a schoolmaster for teaching children that two and two make four, though he does admit that there are times in history "when the man who dares to say that two and two makes four is punished with death." Here we are once again reminded that the power and conviction of Camus' statements about the Plague derive from his own participation in the French Resistance. His modesty is enhanced by the fact that almost daily he wrote editorials for which he could have been tortured and shot. He said that two and two made four, knowing that this was not acceptable to the enemy that occupied his country.

The true touchstone of merit in the kind of action described by Camus is not that it justifies the agent in comparison with other men who have acted less worthily, but that *it communicates the same lucid consciousness to other men and enables them to act in the same way.* It awakens the same "modesty and comprehension" and the same dogged courage—we might say the same "Sisyphean spirit"—a spirit which is satisfied to act on the grounds not of moral good or evil, still less of reward and punishment, but simply as a witness to human truth. "There was nothing admirable about this," says Camus, "it was merely logical." The irony of that sentence is that its logic is rooted not in coherence but in absurdity, and what gives it consistency is not reason but *love.*

Here Camus seems to contradict himself. After all, is not love itself the highest good, the one virtue that gives all other virtues their reality and meaning? He would not deny it. But we must place this thought in its right context. By "virtue," Camus generally refers to what *society considers to be virtue,* that is to say, the normative system of conduct that is preached with a certain amount of fallacious rhetoric. Such virtue is admired by all and practiced by few. It merely sets the tone for forensic condemnations, for moral and political witch hunts, for censorious self-righteousness, and is easily evaded by everyone rich or powerful enough to get away with it. In other words, virtue is for Camus a kind of social disease, an endemic state of hypocrisy and doublethink which he called *la moraline* ("moralitis"). It is a matter of talk, of conventional attitudes, of cliché thinking, and has nothing whatever to do with the classic idea of *virtus.*

The whole satiric theme of *The Stranger,* where the hero is condemned to death as a murderer chiefly on the grounds that he did not weep at his mother's funeral (thereby proving himself a "criminal type"), is that the standards of right and wrong, law and order, virtue and vice upheld by the court, are in fact pure absurdities.

The same irony appears in *The Plague,* but in a much less evident way: the "normal" life of the city retains a certain tranquillity and order by virtue of certain assumptions which break down under the stress of the epidemic. But then they are replaced by other standards, less grandiose, less easy to preach and to praise, but certainly more basic and more real: the standards of men like Rieux, Tarrou, and all the others who sacrifice themselves to save the city. What actually happens, of course, is that instead of the convenient automatic functioning of a social system in which, at the same time, everybody and nobody really participates (all are implicated but few are actually *committed*), there arises a new order of freedom and love in which all who take an active part do so by their own deliberate choice and out of the two motives Camus approves: revolt against the absurdity and arbitrariness of an evil destiny, and determination to give their lives in the affirmation of man, of life, and of love. Those who do not manage to arrive at this solution are either passive and helpless victims of the Plague or, worse still, its accomplices.

Absurdity—Revolt—Love. This whole attitude, which is of course a highly ethical one, is summed up in Camus' *Notebook* of 1946: THUS STARTING FROM THE ABSURD, IT IS NOT POSSIBLE TO LIVE REVOLT WITHOUT REACHING AT SOME POINT OR OTHER AN EXPERIENCE OF LOVE THAT IS STILL UNDEFINED.[8]

This progression is basic in the whole work of Camus. In his early successes (*The Stranger* and *The Myth of Sisyphus*) Camus is exploring the world of the absurd. Those who have never read any other books of his often remain under the impression that Camus was *preaching* the absurd as a way of life. They have an entirely defective view of Camus' real philosophy, especially if they attach too much importance to the "ethic of quantity" which he propounded in some chapters of *Sisyphus* and which he later, quietly, retracted and altered.

The lucid realization of the absurd is, for Camus, only a first step. The function of this lucidity is not simply to negate and to deride the illusory standards of bourgeois society. Still less is it merely a groundwork for an ethic of austere and ironic despair. It is the first step toward a kind of modest hope. *The Myth of Sisyphus* is explicitly directed against suicide. Where one might be tempted to think "because life is absurd, let's get it over with," Camus replies, "because life is absurd that is all the more reason for living, and for refusing to surrender to its absurdity."

Life, then, becomes a revolt against negation, unhappiness, and inevitable death. It is, under these conditions of lucidity and courage, a valid affirmation of freedom: the only freedom man has, the freedom to keep going even though a certain logic might seem to prove that resistance is useless. Camus detects this logic subtly at work in society itself and in the apparent "order" and "truth" by which society lives.

Indeed, what society preaches in *justification* of man's existence usually turns out, upon examination, to be a derisory, almost satanic repudiation of that existence. What society preaches as "the good life" is in fact a systematically organized way of death, not only because it is saturated with what psychologists call an unconscious death wish but also because it actually rests on death. It is built on the death of the nonconformist, the alien, the odd-ball, the enemy, the criminal. It is based on war, on imprisonment, on punitive methods which include not only mental and physical torture but, above all, the death penalty.

The ambiguities of social thinking spring from the fact that while life, joy, love, and peace are theoretically extolled, the machine is actually kept running by murder, greed, violence, hatred, war. This ambiguity is common both to affluent conservative establishments and to revolutionary dictatorships. In either case, the mode of conduct that is extolled as "right" is in fact a covert justification for cruelty, lying, killing—for all the evil and injustice upon which society itself actually rests. All this is discovered by Tarrou when he realizes that his father, a prosecutor, sets his alarm clock and gets up very early on certain days: the days when he goes dutifully to watch his victims perish under the guillotine.

As long as one is content to justify one's existence by reference to these automatically accepted norms, one is in complicity with the absurd, with a murderous society, with death, with "the Plague."

When one comes face to face with absurdity itself, when one confronts the death wish in oneself, the question of suicide arises. He who gives in to the temptation consciously ratifies the absurdity which he has always unconsciously accepted. He dies as a passive victim of an absurd and alienated psychology. His first step toward freedom must be the acceptance of life on an entirely new basis: the affirmation that though the reasons which are supposed to justify existence do not, in fact, justify anything at all, he will go on living anyway as a matter of stubborn "Sisyphean" choice. This first step, this basic revolt against the absurd, this affirmation of freedom, sets man on the right path. After affirming his own life, his own existence, as a fundamental value in itself, he existentially realizes the value of life and existence for others as well. It is here that, in Christian terms, man begins to love others as himself. He is able to experience them as other selves insofar as he has actually *chosen his own life* in opposition to absurdity and death. Thus he also *chooses their lives* in defiance of an absurd philosophy or social system which, at any moment, may decree that they are to be killed in war, executed, exiled, or in some way ostracized, disgraced, and repudiated for defying the generally accepted myths. The steps follow one another with an inexorable "logic" which is, however, not the logic of syllogism but logic based on *choice*. Once this "logic of preference" has experienced the free choice of life as the basic value and the starting point of all action, then it follows: (1) that one must live in constant revolt against an absurd social philosophy which, in one form or other, is nihilistic and based on murder. (2) One must live in solidarity and love with those whom one is ready to defend against the attacks of "the absurd"— against the death drive built into the structure of social existence. One must, in other words, make every effort to build a new order of love to supersede the false order which, for all its ideology of humanitarian love or of supernatural grace, is in fact a justification for murder and for hate. (3) But here the real difficulty begins: How is one to build this new order? Revolution, as Camus shows in *L'homme revolté*, is also a facile justification of mass murder. *Can there be any historic action that does not eventually end in mass murder?*

This was a question which Camus had the honesty not to answer. He admitted that he did not know. But because he did not know, he remained to some extent uncommitted, undecided, and hence to some extent an accomplice of the established disorder. Therefore, what he said about love was ambiguous. Therefore he had to be very "modest" about it indeed. Therefore what he said about it was said almost in an undertone, almost as an aside, though it was in face central to his thought.

Once again we turn to the *Notebooks:*

The end of the absurd, rebellious etc. movement, the end of the contemporary world consequently, is compassion in the original sense; in other words ultimately love and poetry. But that calls for an innocence I no longer have. All I can do is recognize the way leading to it and to be receptive to the time of the innocents. To see it, at least, before dying.[9]

This is a significant passage, because it reflects something of the deep inner struggle with which Camus confronted the work he wanted to do after finishing *The Plague*. He said somewhere that he wanted to get *The Plague* out of his system, "after which I tell myself that I shall write about happiness." And he added, elsewhere, that this meant writing about "a certain kind of love."

The unusual hesitations, the profound moral scruples which kept Camus so often silent and which prevented him from ever fulfilling this intention, are rooted in his sense of lost innocence. The pages in which he best speaks of the love of life, and of an almost Franciscan happiness, are concentrated in his early essays. At the end of his life he was turning back toward these, to recapture the luminous and abandoned innocence of his Mediterranean existence, after the foggy hell of Amsterdam and *The Fall*. He never had time to go back. And one wonders if he ever really expected to. The sense of lost innocence, of complicity in a world of horror which exceeded the power of imagining, remained dominant in Camus up to the end. Yet he confidently looked for others who were innocent. Did he feel that he had lived to see "the time of the innocents"? Those of us who have learned to be deeply moved by the sincerity and the "innocence" of a new generation that remembers nothing of World War II and seeks only to prevent World War III may be inclined to think that Camus, in these words as in so many others, gave evidence of prophetic insight.

Why did Camus not turn to Christianity as a source of hope, an affirmation of life? We shall discuss this in connection with the sermons of Père Paneloux. For the moment, we can content ourselves with saying that, for Camus, the Christian idea of grace had, like that of virtue, become distorted beyond recognition. "Grace" was, in the eyes of Camus, nothing more than the state of smug self-assurance by which the elect convinced themselves of their election. Grace was nothing but the secure self-satisfaction of respectable members of a society that "justified" its basically murderous and destructive activity by means of abstract ethical ideas. "Grace" for Camus was, then, the capacity to adjust without resistance to the demands of an establishment and to believe oneself thereby chosen by God and destined for eternal salvation. Obviously, this is a complete reversal of the Christian doctrine of justification. Yet who can deny that the caricature has, in fact, a basis which has been accurately described by writers like Mauriac, Julien Green, Graham Greene, Flannery O'Connor, J. F. Powers, and others? In any event, the *Notebooks* of Camus ironically observe: "Happy Christians, they kept grace for themselves and left us charity." This was written shortly after the publication of *The Plague*, and it might well refer to the kind of charity practiced by Rieux and Tarrou as "saints without God"—therefore without grace. Once again, the distorted notion of grace must be noted. Like virtue, "grace" here supposes a kind of social justification, a logic of acceptability, an affirmation of *rightness*. What is done out of "grace," in such a case, is justified by the fact that it *proves something beyond itself*. It is not only an act good in itself, but it proves that one is a Christian, or it proves that God exists, or it proves that the establishment is forever right, or it proves curial infallibility, the Immaculate Conception of St. Joseph, or a million other things.

Camus and Kafka. At this point it is essential to discuss, at least briefly, the obvious resemblances between Camus and Kafka. This is made easy for us by the fact that Camus himself devoted a chapter to "Hope and the Absurd in Kafka" in *The Myth of Sisyphus. The Plague* and Kafka's *Castle* have something in common, in that they deal symbolically with the relation between man and the inscrutable powers that influence his destiny without his being able to understand them. The mythical dimension of this relationship is much more elaborate in *The Castle* than in *The Plague*. We need only recall that K. lives as a stranger in the village outside the Castle, insisting that he has been summoned there to work as a surveyor but never able to make any decisive contact with the elusive officials inside the Castle. He never enters the Castle, and wastes his time in an exhausting, fantastic struggle with the Byzantine protocol that governs all communication between the Castle and the village. Obviously Kafka is speaking, in terms at once satirical and tragic, of religious alienation: man's struggle to bridge the gap between himself and a realm of utterly inaccessible transcendence.

It must be clear, of course, that what Kafka describes is man's attempt to imagine and to understand grace in terms of hierarchic organization, that is to say, in terms of "law." For anyone who understands the New Testament, it is clear that this involves a contradiction beyond any solution. But for anyone who knows church history, it is also clear that for most people the contradiction is in fact inevitable. They cannot understand grace in any other terms.

One of the villagers is the girl Amalia, whose whole family is cursed and disgraced because she has refused a most insulting proposition from one of the Castle officials. She is in the right, but in the eyes of the village she has violated a basic moral axiom: the officials of the Castle are always to be obeyed. Faced with a decision between truth to her own integrity and loyalty to a corrupt but accepted "moral" standard, she prefers to do what is regarded as "wrong." She refuses unquestioning obedience to an arbitrary and revolting command. Her act is precisely the kind of choice which Camus describes as "revolt" against the arbitrary and the absurd, in affirmation of one's own personal life, one's own authenticity and existential truth.

Camus' commentary on this is very revealing. It expresses exactly his own critique on conventional notions about "grace," "virtue," and "religion." In his eyes, this is the kind of choice that is forced on one who seeks a transcendent solution to the mysteries of life: he is bidden to renounce his human dignity, his honor, his assertion of his personal truth and worth, and submit blindly to "answers" and "commands" which are an insult to his humanity. His act of submission makes him "worthy of grace." He who has thus surrendered his dignity in a blind act of self-prostration before the unknown has passed the test of faith, has made the "leap" into the dark, and is thereafter "justified." All further activity rooted in this submission is "right" and "good." It is "virtuous" and it "proves something." What? It proves that he is one of the elect, that his relations with the Castle are perfectly correct, and that he has a place in the village (that is to say, in human society).

On the other hand, he who refuses to surrender his human dignity in a blind act of obeisance to what is essentially inhuman becomes a pariah in the village. The morality of Camus demands precisely this refusal.

The ambiguity of Camus' answer is, however, evident to anyone who sees that it is based on a caricature of faith and grace. But let us be quite clear: the caricature cannot be blamed on Camus. Christians themselves are the ones responsible for it. He is simply expressing repugnance for a twisted and degraded form of "Christian morality" which has evolved historically in the framework of a civilization whose social institutions have tended to preserve "Christian values" by embalming them instead of allowing them to renew their own intrinsic life.

Without stopping to clarify this entirely wrong concept of grace, we need only admit once again that it is in fact all too common. But it is, of course, a contradiction of the theological concept of grace. An act which springs from grace is *purely gratuitous* and seeks no justification other than its own gratuitousness, that is to say, its freedom from any limitation, any need for an explanation other than itself. An act that has to be justified by an appeal to something other than its own intrinsic content of love becomes by that fact a legalistic action. It is justified by a norm outside itself.

Camus, without knowing it, was in the thick of the old argument of grace versus the law and, without being aware of the fact, was on the side of grace. He found himself disputing in grace's favor against those who had turned grace into a purely arbitrary law. This is not to say that Camus was a secret Christian, but only that a Christian is free, if he likes, to understand Camus in a Christian sense which Camus himself did not realize.

Rieux and Tarrou. The main characters in *The Plague* are all, in their various ways, solitary people. But their lives are built into a dialectic of solitude and solidarity, of isolation and integrity on the one hand, of commitment, compassion, and love on the other. This is fitting, for the mystery of death is, after all, a mystery of inexorable solitude; and yet it is something shared by everyone. The Plague intensifies this mystery and brings out, in sharp relief, the Camusian problems of the absurd, revolt, compassion, and common action to affirm and protect life against death. Naturally, the two main characters of the book, the "heroes" of the Plague (in the qualified sense we have given to the word hero) are Dr. Rieux and the ironic, lonely Tarrou. The Plague brings them together in a common battle, and both—though Rieux vigorously repudiates the allegation—are in a certain sense "saints without God." Who are they? Or perhaps it would be better to ask, What kind of people are they?

What Camus gives us is not so much detailed history or formal characterization. He portrays his characters two-dimensionally in their attitude toward life and toward the crisis in which they are involved. Yet they are men of flesh and blood, not mere abstractions. Of the two, Rieux is the more massive, more serious being: a man who has known work and suffering and who, as the book opens, has just had to send his wife away to a TB sanitarium, knowing he will probably never see her again. We are introduced to Rieux as a man who is somewhat weary and disillusioned, but firmly committed to the service of other men and to an uncompromising refusal of what he considers dishonest. Serious, reflective, he is not an abstract thinker. In his conflict with the city officials, who are unwilling to accept the fact that the epidemic is really the Plague, he shows himself to be one who starts with facts rather than with definitions. Having determined the facts, he then finds a definition to fit them accurately. He has little patience with the official mind that goes at things the other way round, that starts with a definition of how things are supposed to be and then does all it can to make the facts keep fitting the definition, even when the two have long since parted company.

Ultimately, the difference between the two types of thinking boils down to this: Rieux is concerned with facts because he is interested above all in the needs of living persons. The others are concerned with definitions and legal principles because they are interested above all in the established institutions by which they live.

Rieux is, however, so objective, so reticent, so little inclined to pass judgment, that he is thought by Rambert to be without feeling. Only later does Rambert discover the truth of Rieux's human suffering in his separation from his wife.

Above all, Rieux is the one who sees deepest into the real nature of the Plague and who fully understands what it means for the whole life of the town to become "a dreary struggle between each man's happiness and the abstractions of the Plague." He cannot in any way agree with the theology of Paneloux, who *justifies* the Plague and tries to make people love their sufferings. His criticism of Paneloux has two aspects. First, he does not take him too seriously: *"Christians sometimes talk like that without really thinking it,"* he says. *"They're better than they seem."* A devastating compliment! Second, he reasons that Paneloux is a scholar, and therefore judges evil and suffering in terms of what he has read in his theology books: "That's why he can talk with such assurance of the truth with a capital T. Every country priest . . . who has heard a man gasping for breath on his deathbed thinks as I do. He'd try to relieve human suffering before trying to point out its excellence."

Rieux has the same quarrel with Paneloux that he has with the city officials. Paneloux, he thinks, is more interested in justifying the ways of God to man than in the plight of man himself. In other words, what Paneloux is really interested in—until he learns better from his own experience of the Plague—is proving that his religious establishment is right rather than helping men struggle against the Plague. Rieux is not a believer. Not that he is a militant atheist; he is simply a modern man who does not quite know what so much talk about God can possibly mean. He admits it all leaves him fumbling in the dark, and arguments of men like Paneloux are no help whatever.

Rieux's chief problem with the idea of God is that of innocent suffering. If those who seek to justify God explain suffering by saying it is directly willed by God, then they make God a monster of injustice. Suffering is a punishment for sin? But why should God punish an innocent child who has never sinned? The forensic idea of an original guilt which makes everyone a priori subject to punishment and damnation whether he consciously does any wrong or not, does not satisfy Rieux. He manages, with the help of the Plague, to make Paneloux see the difficulty all too clearly. But is this all? Actually, Rieux has a deeper intuition, shared with Tarrou—a sense that this pessimism about man, this degrading repudiation of man in order to justify the authoritarian image of God, is in reality bound up with a social structure that depends on force, cruelty, prison, death sentences, and war. What the doctrine of evil seeks to justify with its inquisitional fires is not simply the Father Image of God, but the authoritarian social establishment and its cruel laws.

The Plague draws its real power from the death wish and the destructiveness that are built into man's own life. It is not merely a visitation from outer space, a punishing angel sent from heaven. It comes to full view on emerging from its hiding place, the city and its inhabitants. The people's *indifference to life and to authentic values*—an indifference which is justified and enhanced by their ideology and their social mores—*allows the Plague to take undisputed possession of them.* This indifference itself is already an indication of the Plague's dormant presence. Germaine Brée has summed up Camus' idea—which is expressed by Rieux and Tarrou—very succinctly.

Unopposed, [the Plague] organizes all that is bad in human life into a coherent and independent system: pain, death, separation, fear and solitude. And it disorganizes and destroys all that is good: freedom, hope, and most particularly love. . . . The Plague is not the symbol of an outer abstract evil; it merely applies and *carries to their logical limits the values implicit in the unconscious attitudes of the citizens of Oran.*[10]

This makes the Plague an excellent typological device for discussion of Nazism and other absolutisms, which operate in exactly the same way. The power of a dictator and of an authoritarian and violent party is made possible by the attitudes and dispositions already present in the people who submit to it, for in the depths of their hearts they want to submit. That is why, in Camus' eyes, the sermon of Paneloux urging people to submit to the Plague as a just punishment is—like the sermons of French clerics urging acceptance of Nazi rule—simply a form of collaboration with the evil in man, an act of obedience to the innate fury of pestilence and of death. But how can Rieux believe this if he does not also, in some form or other, believe in something remarkably like original sin? This Camus fails to explain.

Tarrou is somewhat less stolid than his friend Dr. Rieux. He is a poet of sorts, a more articulate thinker, more ironic, a "singular man" who is a bit of a poet and who frequents "Spanish dancers." He has a sharp eye for curious and human detail—it is he who observes the old man who likes to spit on cats (a real individual, enshrined in Camus' *Notebooks*). Tarrou is given to understatement. He looks at things through the wrong end of the telescope. He does not believe in heroism—certainly not the heroism of a Malraux, still less of a de Gaulle. Yet he aspires to a kind of sainthood. He wonders if it is possible for him to be a "saint without God." Can he be? He once thought of himself as "innocent." But was he ever in reality innocent? "I had the plague already before coming," he says. His whole history is, he recognizes, a history of Plague.

His father was a prosecutor, and one day in court Tarrou, a boy, suddenly realized what his father was doing: dressed in legal robes, haranguing the jury, demanding the death penalty for a criminal, he was permitting himself to become the incarnation of socially approved blood lust. He was acting as the willing and righteous instrument of a society that delighted in murder, provided the murder could be carried out in socially acceptable ways. Tarrou ran away from home and became a rebel against society: *"The social order around me was based on the death sentence and by fighting the established order I'd be fighting against murder."* But then, Tarrou asks, can one really wash his hands of society and its evil merely by a good intention? Can one become innocent by one's own declaration, backed up by some symbolic gesture (burning a draft card, for example)? This is not a foregone conclusion. The great problem remains to be faced. "We can't stir a finger in the world without the risk of bringing death to somebody." But does that not make all life unlivable?

Once again, if every act of man in involved in murder, one fails to see the difference between the doctrine of Camus and Augustine's pessimism on original sin. Innocence is equally impossible whichever way you look at it. But Tarrou reaches certain practical conclusions. First: it is possible to refuse all conscious and deliberate cooperation in any social action, any doctrine, any policy, whether revolutionary or conservative, which *justifies murder in order to exploit it freely.* In other words, though one cannot avoid all implication in some form of violence (Camus did not believe consistent nonviolent action was possible), one can at least refuse to cooperate with the social machinery of *systematic and self-justifying violence.* One can reject specious ideologies which permit massive killing in war, in pogroms, in nihilistic violence on the grounds of race, religion, class, nationalism, and so forth.

"On this earth," Tarrou declares in words which Camus explicitly made his own elsewhere, "there are pestilences [an early draft has "excutioners"] and victims, and it's up to us, so far as possible, not to join forces with the pestilences."

Starting from this, Tarrou builds his ethic of "comprehension." Indeed, it is more than an ethic, it is almost a monastic ascesis: it demands constant *attention* (compare the old monastic idea of "vigilance" and "custody of the heart"). It is a monastic spirituality of *exile* because he who refuses to cooperate with the "pestilence" which is part and parcel of every social establishment, cannot really be accepted by that establishment. He remains a stranger in his own city. But in that city he nevertheless retains his sympathy for and concern with those whom he sees to be potential or actual victims of hidden plagues. Finally, one can perhaps be a "saint without God" insofar as one does all these things without expecting a reward and without calling on God to justify and approve one's acts.

The expression "saint without God" sounds more anti-Christian than it really is. In fact, the Christian idea of disinterested sanctity is not very remote from this. St. John of the Cross somewhere remarked: "You should do your good actions in such a way that, if it were possible, God himself would not know you were doing them."

As for Rieux, he does not condemn Tarrou's idea, but merely remarks that for his own part, he does not want to be a saint or a hero: what interests him is simply "being a man." And to tell the truth, that is already heroic enough.

Grand, Cottard, and Rambert. Since Grand and Cottard are neighbors, we might as well consider them together. But one is on the side of the angels, the other is with the devils. In other words, Grand is on the side of life, with Rieux and Tarrou. Cottard is on the side of death and the Plague. Why? As the books opens, Cottard has just tried to hang himself. He is wanted by the police. When the Plague comes, all official attention is diverted to the crisis, and the police forget about him. For Cottard, the Plague means freedom, respectability, and even a certain material well-being. He makes money on the black market, goes about in public, visits the cafes, enjoys life. The Plague is his element. He wants it to go on forever. When the statistics begin to promise an improvement, he refuses to believe them. When the Plague finally ends, he goes insane and starts shooting indiscriminately at everything that moves. He is captured by the police and brutally killed. Cottard is the one character in the book who most obviously points to the Nazi occupation. He is a typical "collaborator."

Grand, on the other hand, appears at first sight to be nothing more than a dull, self-important civil servant, a failure in life who tries to console himself by his absurd obsession with writing a novel. But because he is a perfectionist—and not endowed with much creative imagination—he never gets beyond the first sentence, which he rewrites over and over, this way and that, on page after page.

He knows he is getting nowhere, but he keeps working in his spare time, Plague and all, because he dreams of the day when his manuscript will be discovered by a great publishing house, and the editor-in-chief will cry out to all the assembled staff, "Gentlemen, hats off!" This, in Grand's opinion, is what happens in publishing houses when a new masterpiece is discovered!

And yet, for all his failure, for all his devotion to a civil service job that undoubtedly should make him (if Tarrou is right) a collaborator with a murderous system, Grand is nevertheless something of a "hero." Why? Because he is, after all, like Sisyphus. His mild megalomania is no obstacle to this: it fits in. It can be approved. It helps him, in his own way, to revolt against the absurdity of his meaningless existence, because it keeps him valiantly pushing away at his own Sisyphean boulder—the first sentence of an impossible masterpiece.

We can better appreciate the sympathetic character of the journalist Rambert if we contrast him with another character who filled the same position in the first draft of the book and was later eliminated. This character, Stephan, is abandoned by his wife and then, though he survives the Plague, commits suicide. Rambert is totally different, both in his story and in his attitude. He is a completely positive, life-loving character. He is a stranger in Oran, and seeks to escape in order to rejoin his wife, whom he loves passionately. He makes repeated efforts to get out of the city. But finally, when he seems likely to succeed, he changes his mind and decides to remain and help Tarrou and the sanitary squads fight the Plague. In the end, however, he survives the Plague and is reunited with his wife in an almost ecstatic scene at the railway station. This serves as a striking contrast to the loneliness of Rieux, who has lost his wife and his friend Tarrou. But in reality the reunion scene is not altogether consistent with the story, since there is no reason why Rambert's wife should come to the Algerian town. Logic would seem to demand that Rambert go to meet her at their home in France, which is what he has been trying to do all along. Nevertheless, Rambert plays an important part in the artistic structure of the book. As a character he is aesthetically "right": he contrasts with the reflectiveness of Rieux and Tarrou. He is a straight type with healthy and deep impulses, grounded in the love of life and of his woman. He wastes no time in discussion, though he does at times become engaged in the issues raised by the two protagonists. But in the main he moves in a sober and simple world —that of the Spanish soccer player Gonzalez and of the sentries who are supposed to help engineer his escape.

One more minor character must be mentioned. In a book where there are few women—the solitude of men separated from their beloved is one of the emphatic themes of the novel—the whole weight of femininity is carried by Rieux's mother. She does little, she says practically nothing—but she is a "presence." She is there when Tarrou dies. She is a very considerable support for her son in his loneliness and his exhaustion. She remains shadowy, yet is very real: a kind of silent incarnation of the "comprehension" about which Tarrou talks so much. This is the true role of woman in Camus' world: she is there to embody wisdom and love because she is capable of a dimension of understanding that too easily escapes the logic machine which is the active mind of man.

The Bossuet of Oran: Père Paneloux. Finally we come to a character whom the Christian reader cannot help but find a little perplexing. Paneloux tends to polarize the thought of those who fight the Plague at Oran, but himself remains quite ambiguous. What does he finally add up to? The answer is never quite certain, and Camus intended to leave it a mystery. This contributes to the unusual interest of a priest figure that was intended to bear the burden of traditional Christianity and of historical Christendom in a book which blames both for contributing to the modern pestilence. More than that: we shall see that in fact Paneloux bears other burdens as well. At times we hear him echo the justification of evil which Camus, in his university thesis, attributed to the Gnostic Basilides. He explicitly defends the doctrines of Augustine. But in later modifying these, Paneloux ends up with a curiously Nietzschean position. He takes refuge in a pure voluntarism which makes him a kind of Nietz-schean *with* God, just as Tarrou's doctrine of charity without grace tends to make him a saint *without* God. Discussing Nietzsche's last period, Camus, in *L'homme revolté*, attributes to him the same "active fatalism" which he attributes to Paneloux. It would be in-teresting to examine the implications of all this, but space does not permit. At any rate, Paneloux is presented as a "compleat" Jesuit. His voluntarism masks a hidden will to power under a doctrine of total submission to seemingly arbitrary decrees of God.

We have already briefly outlined the two sermons of Paneloux. The first sermon is typical of French classic pulpit oratory—a vibrant, forceful, authoritarian delivery of all the right answers: just the kind of thing that Judge Othon must declare to be "absolutely irrefutable." Paneloux obviously models himself on the great Bossuet, and echoes Bossuet's conservative idea of history. In the beginning, God showed man the difference between right and wrong. Man consistently refused obedience, and history is simply the record of man's infidelities and of the repeated punishments he has to endure as a consequence. The lessons of history are perfectly simple. But when will we ever learn? The Plague gives Paneloux an admirable opportunity to accuse, to judge, and to chastise in the name of God. He does not associate himself with his hearers: he calls them "you." He tells them that *they* have sinned, and that the Plague has been sent to *them* in order to bring them to their senses: the means by which they can effectively do this is to heed his message and fall on their knees.

A better understanding of the power complex behind the first sermon of Paneloux can be gained by a reading of Camus' *The Renegade*. Here the megalomaniac missionary seeks nothing but a chance to affirm his own power by using the word of the gospel to subdue the *most wicked* savages. Ironically, it turns out that the wicked savages are a lot more powerful and persuasive than he, even though they never say anything at all. They just *do:* and what they do is naked evil in its most brutal and uncompromising form. In either case, in *The Renegade* and *The Plague* we find the message of evangelical judgment pitted against straight evil, and evil goes its way in complete indifference. The announcement of judgment and punishment merely serves to reinforce the submission of weak humans to the evil that afflicts them, though that is obvi-ously not the preacher's intention.

Though in the second sermon there is an even stronger emphasis on obedience to the will of God, Paneloux has obviously changed. He has learned a new attitude toward the Plague and toward life itself—indeed, he has almost learned a new attitude toward God. Now he is much humbler—more "modest." Now he does not say "you" to his congregation. He says *we*. He includes himself among the sinners, the sufferers, and above all *among those who do not understand.*

The great difference between the vibrant and irrefutable Bossuet of sermon 1 and the much more chastened preacher of sermon 2 is that the second does not claim to have all the answers. He does not propound a simple view of life and of history that is merely a record of God commanding and man rebelling. He does not conclude that the only solution is "not to rebel." On the contrary, he almost, but not quite, admits that the suffering and death of the innocent boy, Othon's child, have made him hesitate. Not that he has doubted God's existence. He has faced the question of revolt. Is God to be loved or hated? Paneloux no longer dares to solve the problem with a sweeping apologetic argument. He is much more hesitant. Can the answer really be found without any resort to double talk and subterfuge? He no longer trusts formulas, but he has another answer: not of the mind but of the will. It is a question of choice. Either/or. Either one must deny God entirely and reject him entirely, or one must accept *everything*. Love him in everything, including the death of the innocent child. Including one's own death. Including (he hints at this) a sacrifice and death which are apparently without justification, without meaning.

At this point we realize that Paneloux anticipates his own demise and takes upon himself a course of action that is in fact not easy to understand or to justify—his ambiguous death is one that will never merit canonization. His loyalty to the Church is doubted by some of his fellow clerics. Some wonder if his faith has been shaken. But the death of Paneloux is definitely consecrated by an act of stubborn, personal choice.

One element in the choice is clearly bizarre. Paneloux decides that if his faith in God is to be perfectly "pure," he must refuse the aid of a doctor, for to have recourse to human science would be to resist the will of God.

Camus does not say so quite clearly, but we divine that Paneloux, in heroic Christian fashion, has doubtless asked God to lay upon him the punishment of all, all the unrelieved suffering of the worst kind of death by pestilence, and to do this in such a way that Paneloux will receive no praise or credit from men. So, in fact, he dies a mysterious, ambiguous, and stubborn kind of death: he gets precisely what he asks for, whatever it may have been. And, paradoxically, in blindly submitting to God he also manages at the same time to impose his own will on God.

In the tortuous scheme of his own secret, spiritual will to power, Paneloux emerges an absolute winner, but in a victory no one else can possibly find either the time or the casuistic subtlety to comprehend. The implicit conclusion of Camus is that this is the limit of good will which can be expected from a present-day Catholic: an individual drama buried in the solemn and absurd secrecy of a Byzantine, casuistical theory of evil.

Conclusion

Camus, "the conscience of his generation," and indeed of the generation that has followed, is a stumbling block to Christians. He intended to be one. He is a typical "post-Christian" thinker in the sense that he combines an obscure sense of certain Christian values —the lucidity and solidarity of men in their struggle against evil— with an accusatory, satirical analysis of the Christian establishment and of the faithful. His portrait of Paneloux is perhaps bizarre, but it is not pure and simple caricature. One might easily find Christian books—whether of theology or of "spirituality"—which treat the question of evil exactly as it is treated by Paneloux. Admittedly, Paneloux's idea that to consult a doctor would be to resist God is plainly eccentric and erroneous by Catholic standards. Even then, some of the saints have had bizarre ideas and gotten away with them.

But Paneloux is plainly no saint, and we must even admit that his Christianity is defective. Why? Because one looks in vain for any evidence of a really deep human and Christian compassion in this stern, logical mind. He seems to have no authentic Christian sense of mercy, no realization of the love of God for sinful and suffering man, no awareness of divine forgiveness overflowing in the love of man for his brother. Paneloux is learned, he is austere, self-sacrificing, disciplined, and indeed, in a certain sense, heroic. But his heart is sealed off from other men. He is isolated in himself.

Paneloux lives alone with an abstract God, whom he serves with exemplary fidelity, seeking in all things to justify him by logical argumentation and by the stern devotion of an implacable will. The solitude of Paneloux, immured in the stone cell of his own logic and his own will, makes the existential reality of human problems incomprehensible to him. Certainly, he knows that they are problems and he understands his duty to participate in solving them, but this duty itself is abstract. His *idea* of God, his *abstractions* about God, come between him and other human beings. God is therefore not the infinite source of love and forgiveness in whom men are reconciled to one another in charity: he is for Paneloux a cause of opprobrium and of division.

The crisis of the Plague, in which Rieux and Tarrou become spontaneously *united* with others by their unobtrusive service, becomes for Paneloux an occasion for tortuous intellectual problems which, in spite of his good will, eventually cut him off from everyone else. He finally crowns his desperation (which he believes to be "hope") in a bizarre exploit of dying according to some casuistical pattern sanctioned by his own will and offered, for approval, to his inscrutable and abstract Judge.

One of the most shocking sentences uttered by Paneloux is his self-righteous exclamation, when Rieux protests against the "injustice" of the innocent child's death. "Ah," Paneloux sighs, *"now I understand what grace is."* In other words, "Now I know what it is that distinguishes me from this unbeliever here. He cannot see that God is to be loved even when he arbitrarily destroys the innocent. He does not have the grace to believe; consequently he sees only cruelty, and thinks God is wrong. But I have the grace to see that even when he is arbitrary and cruel, God is always right." Grace, then, is that which gives one the ability to submit to a God who acts like an arbitrary tyrant. It gives us the power to submit to a will we do not understand, and even to adore and love what appears horrible. This is an idea that Camus finds revolting. And he is right. It is also an idea which Camus believes to be essential to Christianity, and he is wrong: the idea that God is essentially unjust, and to be loved as such!

Christian faith is not simply the *credo quia absurdum* of Tertullian. Pascal could speak of faith as a wager, and this expression is quite valid in the context of his thought and work: but it is not the last word on all faith and on every problem of the believer.

In other words, faith does not reduce itself always and everywhere into a demand that the believer lovingly and dutifully accept an image of God which is in fact a monstrous and arbitrary theological idol. This perversion of the idea of faith results from an overemphasis on the aspect of authority in faith and from the impasse reached by theological controversy on grace and free will, predestination, and evil since the Reformation. The God of Paneloux may be adorned by Christian terminology, but he is not the God of Christian revelation. He is the perverse abstraction distilled from centuries of futile argument. He is anything but the living God of the prophets, of the New Testament, and of the saints. Indeed, the most awful thing about Paneloux is that he is fanatically loyal to a God that is stone-dead, and the stubborn intensity of his well-meant faith does nothing whatever to bring this idol back to life. People like Paneloux, with their combination of stern rationalism and a dogged will to believe, have brought about the death of God. Camus does not use this expression; he simply finds the God of Paneloux absurd, not because of the exactitude of the theological language about him but precisely because it is only language *about* him. Paneloux has knowledge, discipline, will power, determination, sacrifice, and even a bizarre kind of grace. But he is without love. In portraying him as a Christian without love, Camus is portraying Paneloux as an unchristian Christian. In showing him as a Christian who knows *about* God but obviously does not *know God,* he displays him as a witness to the death of God. The only quarrel we can have with this is to differ with Camus on one point: that *a Christian must inevitably be someone like Paneloux.*

Here a Christian will be likely to suffer a salutary access of Camusian modesty. What one of us can be sure of demonstrating in his life that Camus is not right about Christians? It is a great deal easier, in many ways, to be a Paneloux than it is to be the kind of Christian who will measure up to Camus' exacting standard. But perhaps that is partly due to the fact that we are too self-conscious about ourselves and that, as Christians, we have become more and more habituated to a bad conscience in a world that is fed up with everything about us—not only with our double talk but also with our best efforts at sincerity, not only with our bad faith but also with our flashes of authenticity.

The current apologetic reply to Camus' dismissal of Catholicism goes something like this: Camus was exposed to Augustine when he was not ready for him. He paid too much attention to Pascal and to "sick" Christianity like that of Kierkegaard. And of course he was not favorably impressed by the French Catholic collaborationists and their jeremiads over sin and punishment at the time of the Nazi occupation. But it would have been a different story if Camus had been able to read Teilhard de Chardin.

Is it that easy? To begin with, let us state the question more exactly. It would be impossible to say whether or not Camus, under this or that set of "favorable circumstances," would ever have become "a believer." Such surmises are usually nonsense. The problem with Camus was that he simply could not find Christians with whom he was able completely to *identify himself on every level*. The closest he got was with some of the French priests in the Resistance, and evidently that was not close enough.

What would Camus have liked about Teilhard?

Obviously, first of all, he would have been happy with Teilhard's complete acceptance of nature and of material creation. Teilhard came as close to developing a Christian mystique of matter as anyone has ever done; and Camus, in some of his essays, extols the material, the phenomenal, the sensible, the experience of the fleeting moment, in quasi-mystical language.

A study of Teilhard's writings, and especially of his own spiritual development, shows us to what extent he rebelled against the mentality we have seen in Paneloux: the self-righteous, censorious repudiation of a beautiful world created by God's love. Writing from the trenches in World War I, Teilhard confessed, in a letter to a friend, that even in the midst of war he was meditating and keeping notes on the "real problem of my interior life"—"the problem of reconciling a passionate and legitimate love of all that is greatest on earth, and the unique quest of the Kingdom of Heaven." He explicitly rejects any concept of the world as "only an opportunity to acquire merit." Rather, he sees it as a good creation, coming from the hand of God and given us "to be built up and embellished."

It is of course typical of the spirituality of Paneloux to regard the created world merely as something to be manipulated in order to amass an abstract capital of merit. Paneloux is a spiritual profiteer, and his kind of Christianity is a reflection of the social establishment, with which it exists in a symbiotic unity. Of such Christianity, Teilhard says that it makes one less than a man and a traitor to the human race. Those who observe it from the outside are repelled and "blame my religion for it." That is precisely what Camus does in his portrait of Paneloux.

Teilhard's criticism of this false supernaturalism is that in trying to divert man's capacity to love and turn it aside from concrete human reality to the purely abstract and spiritual, it deadens and distorts man. "The capacity to love cannot with impunity be dissociated from its object: if you try, mistakenly, to cut off our affectivity from love of the universe, are you not in danger of destroying it?" This is what has happened to Paneloux: a good, sincere, strong-willed man, with a strong tendency to intellectualize, he has fallen a victim to an abstract and inhuman spirituality. His power of love has atrophied. His affectivity has been channeled into will-to-power and rigid authoritarianism. When he tries to recover the warmth of love, he ends in a self-immolation which is part heroism and part algebra, an irrefutable conclusion to an argument which no one is able to understand.

Teilhard, on the contrary, wants to transform and divinize the human passions themselves. "I shall put the intoxication of pagan pantheism to Christian use, by recognizing the creative and formative action of God in every caress and every blow. . . . I would like to be able to love Christ passionately . . . *in the very act of* loving the universe." And he asks: "Is there communion with God through the Earth, the Earth becoming like a great Host in which God would be contained for us?"

Camus' basic sympathy for the element of Greek *theoria* in Mediterranean culture would incline him to accept this "Christian gnosis" up to a point. He could identify with the "passionate love," if not with the theological elaboration. Teilhard also completely accepts *man;* and the God of Teilhard is not simply a remote judge and creator, but a God who seeks to complete his epiphany in the world of man by bringing all humanity to convergence and unity in himself, in the Incarnation. The Incarnation for Teilhard is, then, not just an expedient to take care of sin and bring the kind of "grace" that Paneloux was happy about. The Incarnation is ultimately the full revelation of God, not just in man but in the "hominization" of the entire material world.

Camus would have heartily agreed with Teilhard's love of man and with his aspiration toward convergence and human unity. But it is rather doubtful that he would have been able to accept the evolutionary and historical scheme of Teilhardian soteriology. To be precise, it is likely that Camus would have had a certain amount of trouble with the systematic progress of the world toward "hominization" and "christification" by virtue of laws immanent in matter and in history.

The point cannot be adequately discussed here, but anyone who wants to investigate it further had better read Camus' book on revolt (*L'homme revolté*), which he wrote after *The Plague* and which he thought out at the same time as *The Plague*. This study of revolt, which precipitated the break between Camus and the Marxists (especially with Sartre), is a severe critique of Hegelian and post-Hegelian doctrines which seek the salvation and progress of man in the "laws of history."

Camus was suspicious of the way in which totalitarians of both the left and the right consistently appealed to evolution to justify their hope of inevitable progress toward a new era of the superman. In particular, he protested vigorously against their tendency to sacrifice man as he is now, in the present, for man as he is supposed to be, according to the doctrine of race or party, at some indefinite time in the future. In Camus' eyes, this too easily justified the sadism and opportunism of people who are always prepared to align themselves on the side of the executioners against the victims. In other words, a certain superficial type of eschatological hopefulness, based on evolution, made it easy to ignore the extermination camps, the pogroms, the genocide, the napalm, the H-bombs that so conveniently favored the survival of the fittest, got rid of those who no longer had a right to exist, and prepared the way for the epiphany of superman.

At this point, it must be admitted that one of the most serious criticisms of Teilhard bears precisely on this point: an optimism which tends to look at existential evil and suffering through the small end of the telescope. It is unfortunately true that Teilhard, like many other Christians, regarded the dead and wounded of Hiroshima with a certain equanimity as inevitable by-products of scientific and evolutionary progress. He was much more impressed with the magnificent scientific achievement of the atomic physicists than he was with the consequences of dropping the bomb. It must be added immediately, however, that the physicists themselves did not all see things exactly as he did. The concern of Niels Bohr and his dogged struggle to prevent the atomic arms race put him with Rieux and Tarrou, in the category of "Sisyphean" heroes who are

entirely congenial to Camus. After the Bikini test, Teilhard exclaimed that the new bombs "show a humanity which is at peace both internally and externally." And he added beatifically, *"They announce the coming of the Spirit on earth [l'avenir de l'Homme]."*
No matter how much we may respect the integrity and the nobility of this dedicated Jesuit, we have to admit here that in at least one respect he resembles his confrère Paneloux. True, they are at opposite extremes of optimism and pessimism; but they do concur in attaching more importance to an abstract *idea,* a *mystique,* a *system,* than to man in his existential and fallible reality here and now. This is precisely what Camus considers to be the great temptation. Lured by an ideology or a mystique, one goes over to the side of the executioners, arguing that in so doing one is promoting the cause of life.

There is no question whatever that Teilhard believes in the "new man," the *homo progressivus,* the new evolutionary leap that is now being taken (he thinks) beyond *homo sapiens.* Science certainly gives us a basis for hope in this development, and perhaps Camus needed more hope in the future of man than he actually seems to have had. Perhaps Camus was too inclined to doubt and hesitate. Perhaps his "modesty" tended too much to desperation. Perhaps there was much he could have learned from Teilhard. But it is not likely that he would purely and simply have agreed with Teilhard's statement, made in Peking in 1945, that the victorious armies of Mao Tse-tung represented "the humanity of tomorrow" and "the generating forces and the elements of planetization," while the bourgeois European world represented nothing but the garbage (*le déchet*) of history. No doubt there may be good reason to think that a "new humanity" will arise out of the emerging "Third World." Let us hope that it will. But Camus would not be so naïve as to identify this "new humanity" with a particular brand of Marxism, or to pin his hopes on a party which announced its own glorious future as a dogma of faith.

Both Camus and Teilhard firmly took their stand on what they considered to be the side of *life.* Both saw humanity confronted with a final choice, a "grand option," between the "spirit of force" and the "spirit of love," between "division" and "convergence." Man's destiny is in his own hands, and everything depends on whether he chooses life and creativity or death and destruction. Teilhard's scientific mystique and long-range view, extending over millennia, naturally did not delay overlong to worry about the death of a few thousands here and there. Camus could still pause and have scruples over the murder of an innocent child. He refused to justify that death in the name of God. He also refused to justify it by an appeal to history, to evolution, to science, to politics, or to the glorious future of the new man.

Notes

1. Maurice Cranston, in *Encounter* (Feb. 1967).
2. Albert Camus, *Notebooks*, I (New York: Alfred A. Knopf, 1963), p. 193.
3. *Ibid.*, p. 197.
4. Albert Camus, *The Plague* (New York: Alfred A. Knopf, 1948), p. 35.
5. *Ibid.*, p. 38.
6. *Notebooks*, II (New York: Alfred A. Knopf, 1965), p. 158.
7. *The Plague*, p. 121.
8. *Notebooks*, II, p. 138.
9. *Ibid.*, p. 157.
10. Germaine Brée, *Camus* (New Brunswick, N.J.: Rutgers University Press, 1961, rev. ed.), p. 118.

The Waste Land, Ash Wednesday, and Four Quartets

An Introduction and Commentary

FOR readers of twentieth-century literature, the name T. S. Eliot will always be associated with poetic and dramatic innovations. Claimed by both the United States and England, Thomas Stearns Eliot reflected both his American roots and his British orientation in his writing, yet he was bound by neither literary tradition.

About the Poet

Eliot was born in 1888 in St. Louis, Missouri. His father was a prosperous businessman, son of the founder of the first Unitarian church in St. Louis. Religious and educational interests dominated the life of the Eliot family. They were closely associated with the establishment and development of Washington University, and the family circle was enriched by the intellectual stimulus provided by their friends from the university faculty.

Young Thomas Eliot spent an uneventful boyhood in the St. Louis home, with annual visits to Massachusetts relatives. In retrospect, he confessed that he had always been a New Englander in the Southwest and a Southwesterner in New England. The New England ties were strengthened when he followed his years at Smith Academy, a preparatory school for Washington University, with a final preparatory year at Milton Academy before entering Harvard. At Harvard, Eliot was more interested in philosophy than in literature, although his wide reading included classical and modern French literature as well as traditional selections. His philosophical studies covered not only the idealism of the day but also Eastern philosophies. In preparatory school, Eliot had contributed verse to the school paper, and at Harvard he also submitted poems to the undergraduate literary magazine, *The Harvard Advocate*, whose editorship he assumed in his last college year.

Continuing graduate work in philosophy at Harvard, Eliot was granted a traveling fellowship for study at the University of Marburg. The year was 1914; Eliot, like so many other young intellectuals of the period, experienced a sudden shift of plans. He left Germany for Oxford, where he read Greek philosophy at Merton College. Perhaps because of the war, perhaps because of personal affinity, Eliot remained in England and began strengthening the ties that were to mold his life to the British pattern. In 1915 he married Vivienne Haigh-Wood, and later in the year began teaching at Highgate School, near London. Teaching was soon abandoned for more lucrative work, and from 1917 until 1925 Eliot worked as a clerk in Lloyds Bank.

The most important event for Eliot in his first years in England was his meeting with Ezra Pound, who proved to be both a discerning critic and a persevering supporter determined to find a publisher for Eliot's "Prufrock" and other early poems. Despite the disruptive atmosphere of the war and postwar years and the internal crises of a sick wife and an unhappy marriage, Eliot produced some of his most remarkable poetry in his first decade in England. In 1922, "The Waste Land" appeared in the first issue of *The Criterion*, a literary journal edited by Eliot. Although most of Eliot's earlier verse had been startlingly untraditional, it was "The Waste Land" which brought him to the attention of the literary public and marked him as an innovator worthy of note. While experimenting with new forms and structures in poetry, Eliot was also developing as a literary critic and editor; nevertheless, he continued to work as a clerk in the foreign department of Lloyds Bank. In 1925, however, he was able to leave Lloyds and join the publishing firm of Faber and Gwyer (later Faber and Faber). Here he not only found an atmosphere congenial to creative thought and writing, but he also was able to enlarge his circle of literary friends.

For Eliot, 1927 was a time of decision, for in this year he became a British subject and a member of the Anglican Communion. The years immediately following his new allegiance in church and state were years of growing literary recognition, of increasing family tension as his wife's illness became a more acute problem, and of continued work with Faber and Faber. In this period some of Eliot's best-known works were published: *Journey of the Magi, A Song for Simeon, Ash Wednesday, Sweeney Agonistes, Murder in the Cathe-*

dral, and *Family Reunion.* Both the subjects and form of much of his writing during these years reflected his interest in Christian tradition; cadences of the liturgy, cycles in the church year, and episodes in the history of the Church were incorporated in his verse and drama.

Four Quartets, published in 1943, was the consummation of Eliot's poetic art and the fullest portrayal of his philosophical and religious concepts. Three verse dramas were published after *Four Quartets: The Cocktail Party, The Confidential Clerk,* and *The Elder Statesman.* Other minor works also appeared, but the two greatest achievements of Eliot's poetic career remain *The Waste Land* and *Four Quartets.*

Eliot's last years, although less productive for the literary world, were probably the most satisfying of his life. His wife died and his marriage to Valerie Fletcher in 1957 brought him a happiness and fulfillment before unknown to him. Although failing health curtailed his lecturing and traveling, Eliot continued his contacts with authors and critics. He never withdrew from the world of letters until the final withdrawal by death in January, 1965.

Introduction to The Waste Land

When we approach *The Waste Land,* we find that we need to be prepared to enter a world of myth and contemporary realism, of familiar allusions and strange images, of sterile existence and death with glimmers of rebirth. When the poem appeared in the 1920's, critics saw it as a picture of the devastation of war and the desolation of postwar life. Later readers, however, find it speaks of much more than the external ruins of World War I. As the "waste land" experience of modern man, the poem assumes a larger dimension. A first encounter with *The Waste Land* usually evokes feelings of confusion and veiled hope for our despair.

In an anthropological framework structured from fertility myths and ancient Grail legends, the poem explores the meaning of life and death from several planes of experience. The elemental Grail story relates the plight of the lands of the Fisher King, made barren because of a curse due to the King's being sexually maimed. Restoration can come only through magical and superhuman efforts of a knight able to break the spell through his quest for the Grail, or his asking the right question about its meaning. The legend serves as an effective organizational design for Eliot's portrayal of individual and universal sterility, of death-in-life existence.

The landscape of *The Waste Land* is varied: the desert and London's inner city, the luxuriant boudoir and the working girl's dismal flat, the River Thames and the Ganges. Yet, in spite of differences in place and time, barrenness, isolation, meaninglessness, and death dominate the scenes.

The opening section, "Burial of the Dead," provides the question through which the entire poem can be approached. Our traditionally joyful response to spring is challenged in the opening lines by the suggestion that the dormant existence of winter may be preferable to renewed life. Thus, right at the beginning of the poem we are faced with the basic question of the significance of life itself. As the different scenes unfold in the succeeding sections, the question confronts us again. The existence described embodies brokenness and fear, and when there is an effort to seek for meaning and direction in life, the guidance is sought in the wrong place. Madame Sosostris, a clairvoyante, is looked to for counsel, but her wisdom resides in her pack of Tarot cards. Her visions reinforce the sense of fear and meaninglessness in life that are foundational in the poem. Death by water and "crowds of people walking around in a ring," in an endless, unbroken circle bring foreboding. The cyclic crowds again appear in the final portion of "Burial of the Dead." Here they are masses flowing over London Bridge each morning, enmeshed in the endless routine of work days. Ambiguity in the "Stetson" lines of this section allows for varied interpretation, but whatever specific meaning may be associated with the corpse and its sprouting, the motif of life and death is apparent.

"A Game of Chess," the second section of *The Waste Land*, focuses on the problem of relationships in all walks of life. The first episode depicts a nervous, petulant woman in an opulent boudoir. Her staccatolike demands and anxious questions reveal her frustrated, meaningless life. Neither the opulence of her environment nor her companion provides her satisfaction. Her complaining,

> "Speak to me. Why do you never speak. Speak.
> "What are you thinking of? What thinking? What?
> "I never know what you are thinking. Think."

brings a silent response of "I think we are in rats' alley/Where the dead men lost their bones." To the questions, "What shall we do to-morrow. What shall we ever do?" the answer is given:

> The hot water at ten.
> And if it rains, a closed car at four.
> And we shall play a game of chess,
> Pressing lidless eyes and waiting for a knock upon the door.

The monotony of life, the predetermined action as in chess, the hope for a break in the pattern, even if it be the interruption of death—all reflect the conditions of meaningless existence.

The second episode in "A Game of Chess" presents another picture of distorted, loveless relationships. The setting is in exaggerated contrast to the luxurious boudoir of the first section. Cockney women in a London pub discuss problems in the relationship of Lil and Albert. The reference to Lil's abortion suggests the worthlessness of life, and the tenor of the entire conversation limits love to physical passion.

The couples in "A Game of Chess" illustrate distorted relationships and meaningless existence as a universal condition experienced on all social levels. In both episodes, we see the frustration and isolation of sex without love.

Section III, "The Fire Sermon," is a further portrayal of the predicament of man in a world where the significance of life is questioned and where individuals are of worth only in terms of their usefulness to another. By fusion of time and place, Eliot universalizes the desolation of living when the ideal has been replaced by an actuality of decay and seduction. The romantic Thames becomes the river of filth and debris. The Fisher King is now in the contemporary world with a background of a London gashouse, rat-infested canal banks, and city traffic (including trips of the vulgar Sweeneys to the Mrs. Porters). Even the idyllic sound of the nightingale signifies corruption because of its association with the myth of Philomela's violation by Tereu. The unreal city becomes the secular city supporting merchants and methods of questionable repute. Following these illustrations of corruption, Tiresias, the blind seer, is introduced. Timeless, ambisexual, fusing the past with the present, he is the pivotal figure through whose vision the poem may be viewed. In his note Eliot comments, "What Tiresias sees, in fact, is the substance of the poem." The immediate episode recorded by Tiresias is that of the seduction of the typist by "the young man carbuncular." This is another example of sex without love, of a meaningless relationship in a world that seems to offer no meaning. The individuals depicted are characterized by indifference to each other and to the act of violation.

An interlude recording the fellowship at a bar in Lower Thames Street is a happy contrast to the sordid scene in the typist's flat. Here the real city is shown to provide the possibility of meaning and community. The interlude is brief, however, and is followed by songs of the violated Thames maidens. Their songs record episodes from different eras, but the experience is the same. Like the typist, the singers treat their loss of chastity as inevitable and as an inherent part of their existence in the meaninglessness of the waste land. After all, if life itself has no significance, why should traditional patterns of relationship have meaning?

The final lines of section III bring us back to the title, "The Fire Sermon," and bring into focus the central theme of all the episodes.

> To Carthage then I came
>
> Burning burning burning burning
> O Lord Thou pluckest me out
> O Lord Thou pluckest
>
> burning

The cry "O Lord Thou pluckest me out" suggests a solution for the burning of lust. Eliot's notes indicate that the way of asceticism, whether East or West, is implied by the allusions of St. Augustine and Buddha.

"Death by Water," part IV, is a brief interlude between the first three and final sections of *The Waste Land*. It is fitting that "Death by Water" should follow the burning lust of "The Fire Sermon." Knowing Eliot's use of myths in the poem, we might expect to find here the rebirth theme of the drowning fertility gods. However, death alone pervades the scene; rebirth is not even implied. The last lines remind us of the brevity and finality of life.

The opening lines of the concluding section, "What the Thunder Said," suggest the betrayal, trial, and death of Christ. The familiar allusion is allowed by the confusing lines:

He who was living is now dead
We who were living are now dying
With a little patience

Perhaps Eliot is referring to the period between Christ's death and resurrection, or perhaps he is intimating that all gods of death and rebirth—Egyptian, Greek, or the Christ—are not alive to the modern world.

Following the introductory portion, "What the Thunder Said" moves to a description of aridity and sterility that is more bleakly despairing than any of the previous passages. In the portrayal of parched rock and consuming dryness, there is no hope of water. Remembrance of past rains and desire for refreshing relief pervade the passage, yet it concludes, "But there is no water."

Against this mood of finality moves the illusive figure of Christ on the Emmaus road. The allusion is inescapable, but brings with it no sense of refreshment or relief. Instead it leads into a passage of destruction and decay—war, touching many eras and places; chaotic scenes and sounds; "empty cisterns and exhausted wells." The emptiness and decay focus on the Grail Chapel, deserted and "only the wind's home." The Chapel Perilous has its origin in the ancient Grail legends, where it served as a test to the young knight, actually as a part of an initiation rite. In *The Waste Land*, the test of the chapel experience is ended by the cock's crow, which announces the coming rains.

As if to universalize the image of the desolation of life apart from renewal, Eliot introduces a scene of a premonsoon Indian jungle. In this setting, phrases from the Upanishads are introduced: "*Datta, Dayadhvam, Damyata,*" (Eliot's notes translate the terms as "give, sympathize, control"). In their context in the "Fable of the Thunder" in the Upanishads, the words are the answers of the supreme Lord of Creation to the request of his children that he speak to them.

The response of the protagonist to the command "give" is one of self-examination, asking, "What have we given?" His answer reflects a familiar Eliot emphasis on surrender or commitment.

The awful daring of a moment's surrender
Which an age of prudence can never retract
By this, and this only, we have existed

The second command, "sympathize," calls forth a response built on the result of the command "give." The act of surrender is an attempt to break the bonds of personal isolation, a prerequisite for sympathy

> . . . I have heard the key
> Turn in the door once and turn once only
> We think of the key, each in his prison
> Thinking of the key, each confirms a prison

The final command, "control," is answered by the picture of a boat sailing on calm seas and responding gaily to the skilled hands guiding it. A human parallel is drawn in:

> . . . your heart would have responded
> Gaily, when invited, beating obedient
> To controlling hands

The stages of relationship leading to this obedient response to control have been indicated in the "give" and "sympathize" lines. The conditions of surrender and sympathy make possible a gay obedience to "controlling hands."

In the concluding lines, the protagonist sits upon the shore (again the Fisher King figure) with the arid plain behind him. Apparently the curse has not been removed and sterility is still upon the land. As the questor he has been unable to offer the affirmative response to "Give," "Sympathize," "Control," and so has failed the test that would remove the curse. Against this background, he asks a personal question, "Shall I at least set my lands in order?" In response to his question, varied memories come to him: The children's song of London Bridge falling down; Arnaut's leaping back into the refining purgatorial fire (in Dante's *Purgatorio*); a phrase from *Pervigilium Veneris* asking, "When shall I become like the swallow?"; a line about the disinherited Prince of Acquitaine from de Nerval's *El Desdichado*. These are the "fragments shored against his ruins." Although the fragments represent the broken and distorted, they also include suggestions of restoration and renewal. Arnaut's purgatorial flame promises final redemption; *Pervigilium Veneris* is a song of spring and fulfillment. Like the disinherited Prince of Acquitaine in his ruined tower, the protagonist may resolve to recover and rebuild his heritage. The final literary reference, "Why then Ile fit you. Hieronymo's mad againe" (from Kyd's *Spanish Tragedy*), is ambiguous. Perhaps it suggests that the protagonist's acceptance of rebirth and renewal would seem as strange to the contemporary world as did Hieronymo's madness. Perhaps we are to understand that we may be "fitted" for our own quest through exploring the patterns and demands of the poem. The final lines repeat the commands from "What the Thunder Said": "Datta, Dayadhvam, Damyata" (Give, Sympathize, Control), but concludes with a benediction as the fulfillment by the commands, "Shantih, shantih, shantih" (The peace which passeth understanding).

As we survey our journey through *The Waste Land*, we realize that in the shifting scenes and juxtapositions in time we have been confronted with the same basic questions of meaning. We have faced the question of the meaning of our existence as individuals, alone and in relationship, and we have explored our ways of life in a world of death and despair.

Introduction to Ash Wednesday

As Eliot has declared, "we do not cease from exploration" and under his guidance we move on from the "waste land" experience in our quest for meaning. *Ash Wednesday* can be understood as a means of discovery in our search for significance in our existence.

Although the sections of *Ash Wednesday* were published at different times, the poem is a cohesive whole. The title itself is significant, for it connotes the contrition and penitence associated with Ash Wednesday in the Christian tradition. Both Dantean influences and teachings of St. John of the Cross on purgation and renunciation are prominent in the poem. The opening lines, using the cadence of a litany, create a mood of resignation.

> Because I do not hope to turn again
> Because I do not hope
> Because I do not hope to turn
> Desiring this man's gift and that man's scope
> I no longer strive to strive towards such things
> (Why should the agèd eagle stretch its wings?)
> Why should I mourn
> The vanished power of the usual reign?

Viewed in the Ash Wednesday context, these lines suggest that the penitent has no intention of turning again to the old life. In the process of self-emptying and negation, even creative striving is renounced. Here is the "Dark Night of the Soul" experience shared by St. John of the Cross, wherein at this first stage, the soul has renounced the past, and the world, but has no assurance of anything to replace that which it surrendered. Thus, the soul finds no relief or comfort in either the physical or spiritual realm. With the thought of turning from old ways as a part of the process of renunciation, the last lines of the stanza have a clearer meaning. Thus to "mourn the vanished power of the usual reign" would be regression on the way of purgation and renewal.

The mood of resignation continues in the second stanza.

> Because I do not hope to know again
> The infirm glory of the positive hour
> Because I do not think
> Because I know I shall not know
> The one veritable transitory power
> Because I cannot drink
> There, where trees flower, and springs flow, for there is
>   nothing again

The protagonist not only has no hope of restoration by old ways, but has lost all capacity for renewal. His experience is that of encountering nothing.

In the third stanza, the speaker recognizes the restrictive element in time and place and seems unable to discover anything transcendent. The next step in renunciation follows:

> I renounce the blessèd face
> And renounce the voice

Here even the spiritual guide, the one who could offer hope is renounced. The refrain, "Because I cannot hope to turn again," brings the response, "Consequently I rejoice, having to construct something Upon which to rejoice." With this final act of renunciation, that of the blessed face, the struggle of surrender seems resolved.

In the last stanzas of this first poem of *Ash Wednesday,* the penitent turns to prayer, seeking mercy, and freedom from too much self-examination. Recognizing his limitations, the wings that no longer fly, he prays that he may be taught "to care and not to care"; that is, to discern the right goal and to disregard all other interests. "Teach us to sit still" is a petition for submission and for interior quietness such as is advocated by the mystics. The closing lines from the "Ave Maria"—"Pray for us sinners now and at the hour of our death/Pray for us now and at the hour of our death"— focus the poem on the Ash Wednesday theme of suffering and contrition.

Throughout this part of *Ash Wednesday*, there is ambiguity in the meaning of specific sections; nevertheless, there is a cohesive mood of renunciation which gives unity to the whole section and provides a foundation for the following parts of *Ash Wednesday*.

The second poem of the sequence opens with a salutation to the Lady, in which the protagonist recounts an apocalyptic vision suggesting the life-through-death theme. The startling leopard imagery of the vision has been interpreted through varied literary roots, and Eliot, in his skilful use of synthesis, has doubtless drawn from many sources.

Surely, the leopard image suggests total annihilation of the physical self. The struggle of renunciation in the first poem has yielded to acceptance of death itself. The parts of the body devoured by the beasts may represent the centers of physical, emotional, sensual, and intellectual temptation. If so, the details contribute further to the picture of total destruction undergone in the process of renewal. The Ezekiel passage of the valley of dry bones, used earlier in *The Waste Land*, reappears here. The response to God's question, "Shall these bones live?" clarifies the role of the Lady as both spiritual guide and reconciling intermediary between the speaker and the Virgin.

> . . . And that which had been contained
> In the bones (which were already dry) said chirping:
> Because of the goodness of this Lady
> And because of her loveliness, and because
> She honours the Virgin in meditation,
> We shine with brightness. And I who am here dissembled
> Proffer my deeds to oblivion, and my love
> To the posterity of the desert and the fruit of the gourd.

In the response, there is evidence also of a different understanding of death. Out of dry bones comes chirping, a sign of life, and the appearance of the bones is shining brightness. This handling of the dead bones symbol is in direct contrast to that of earlier Eliot poems where it signified the threat of sterility, death, and extinction. In proffering of "deeds to oblivion" and "love to the posterity of the desert," there is further indication of willing renunciation of the most fundamental elements in life, the creative work of mind and strength, and the sharing of the self. In this, all pride would be abandoned. The next lines suggest that restoration can come from the residuum rejected by the devouring leopards, perhaps possible only because of the previous relinquishing of pride. A return to the Lady pictures her as withdrawn in contemplation, and dressed in white, a symbol of purity and righteousness. Whiteness is also seen in the bones as an atoning symbol, atoning "to forgetfulness." The protagonist's desire to forget all but his consuming purpose (purgation) is expressed as,

> ... As I am forgotten
> And would be forgotten, so I would forget
> Thus devoted, concentrated in purpose. ...

Following this declaration of self-negation comes the word from God to prophesy to the wind. To this the chirping bones respond in a litany of praise to the Lady. Here the Lady merges into the figure of the Virgin as she is extolled as the consummation of all human desiring, the fulfillment of all striving, the final end and goal.

In the concluding lines of the second poem, the mood of praise and joy continues. The bones, although still scattered, declare they are glad to be scattered. The sand of the desert is still present, but has been transformed to a blessing; the desert itself is no longer a threat, but a place of quietness. This is acknowledged as an inheritance which is accepted as good.

The third poem of *Ash Wednesday* opens with the theme of turning found in part one. However, turning here differs from that of the first section. The emphasis now is on turning *toward* in the upward struggle, rather than turning *from* in initial renunciation. In the ascent, there are reminders of earlier temptations. Although there is continuing progress on the upward way, there are also impediments of old memories and new phases of darkness. The distraction of earthly beauty, of the recurring struggle between hope and despair, is answered by the penitent's prayer of confession.

> Lord, I am not worthy
> Lord, I am not worthy
>> but speak the word only.

The fourth poem opens with an unnamed figure in a dreamlike atmosphere. By the descriptive detail provided, it may be surmised that this is either the Lady of the previous poems, or another who, like her, has special spiritual significance as guide or mediator. She has both human and divine characteristics, "talking of trivial things" yet having "knowledge of eternal dolour." She seems to give power, freshness, soothing coolness, and firmness even in the realm of nature. To the protagonist, she comes as one whom he has known before, in some earlier epiphany. And in her coming, she brings back memories of the past, which through her can have new meaning.

> Here are the years that walk between, bearing
> Away the fiddles and the flutes, restoring
> One who moves in the time between sleeping and waking,
>> wearing
>
> White light folded, sheathed about her, folded.
> The new years walk, restoring
> Through a bright cloud of tears, the years, restoring
> With a new verse the ancient rhyme. Redeem
> The time. Redeem
> The unread vision in the higher dream
> While jewelled unicorns draw by the gilded hearse.

Thus she comes, restoring the past to the present, giving meaning to time and understanding to vision. This thought is continued in the final lines.

> The silent sister veiled in white and blue
> Between the yews, behind the garden god
> Whose flute is breathless, bent her head and signed but
>> spoke no word

But the fountain sprang up and the bird sang down
Redeem the time, redeem the dream
The token of the word unheard, unspoken

Till the wind shake a thousand whispers from the yew

And after this our exile

Here is not only the vision of one who could guide through the sign of the cross, but also the foreshadowing of the Incarnate Word ("The token of the word unheard, unspoken").

In the light of this high vision, this glimmer of reality, death may seem "enviable and life an exile." So ends the poem, with a fragment from "Salve Regina": "And after this our exile," which may suggest to the reader the concluding words of the prayer: ". . . show unto us the blessed fruit of thy womb, Jesus."

The theme of the Incarnate Word, introduced in the fourth poem, is developed in the fifth poem. The protagonist considers the question of why the Word has not been received, why it has been lost to the world. He concludes that it is present in the world even though it is unrecognized and that it is, in fact, the center of the world. The prologue of the Fourth Gospel is reflected in the first stanza in,

Still is the unspoken word, the Word unheard,
The Word without a word, the Word within
The world and for the world;
And the light shone in darkness and
Against the Word the unstilled world still whirled
About the centre of the silent Word.

The response "O my people, what have I done unto thee" represents the voice of the Lord in Micah 6:3, and the word of Christ in the Reproaches of the Good Friday liturgy. The refrain as used here suggests that God challenges man to question why the Word is rejected. Furthermore, it declares the reconciling word in the reminder of the God-to-man relationship in the "O my people."

In the second stanza the protagonist continues to consider the resistence to the Word. His explanation of the problem echoes the biblical image of walking in darkness, and reintroduces the "face" and "voice" of the first poem. Here, however, there is no sacrificial renunciation, but rather avoidance and denial of these symbols of the spiritual.

The third and fourth stanzas elaborate the phrase "those who walk in darkness." The phrase is used to describe those torn between conflicting spiritual and physical drives, those struggling to make the final surrender.

> Those who are torn on the horn between season and
> season, time and time, between
> Hour and hour, word and word, power and power, . . .

The protagonist confesses his need in his cry, "Will the veiled sister pray for/ Those who walk in darkness . . . ," and again,

> . . . Will the veiled sister pray
> For the children at the gate
> Who will not go away and cannot pray:
> Pray for those who chose and oppose

The final word is that of the Lord, a fragment of the earlier response, "O my people."

In this portion of *Ash Wednesday*, the desert and darkness recur as images of estrangement. The garden, often a symbol of the reconciled state, is here presented in relation to the desert.

> In the last desert between the last blue rocks
> The desert in the garden the garden in the desert
> Of drouth, . . .

The interpenetration of the two images suggests that alienating factors remain in reconciliation; and that even within estrangement there is the possibility of reconciliation.

The opening of the final poem of *Ash Wednesday* repeats the opening lines of the first poem, with the first word of each line altered. The struggle of dying and rebirth remains, but the mood of the poem is one of acceptance free from disillusion. The beauty of the natural world still has an appeal for the penitent, although he has willed total renunciation. However, he seems to accept as a part of the process of purgation the repeated temptations to turn back to sensuous satisfactions. The nostalgic description of sea and countryside suggests the struggle involved in surrendering the memories of the past as well as in controlling present desire.

And the lost heart stiffens and rejoices
In the lost lilac and the lost sea voices
And the weak spirit quickens to rebel
For the bent golden-rod and the lost sea smell
Quickens to recover
The cry of quail and the whirling plover
And the blind eye creates
The empty forms between the ivory gates
And smell renews the salt savour of the sandy earth

This is the time of tension between dying and birth
The place of solitude where three dreams cross

Eliot seems to refer to the place where dreams cross when he wants to indicate a place of decision. Here, as elsewhere, he struggles with the significance of the decisive moment, the moment of dying and rebirth. However, his struggle is tempered by his awareness of a spiritual guide, the feminine figure who fulfills the role of priestly intermediary. The protagonist prays,

Blessèd sister, holy mother, spirit of the fountain, spirit
of the garden,
Suffer us not to mock ourselves with falsehood
Teach us to care and not to care
Teach us to sit still
Even among these rocks,
Our peace in His will
And even among these rocks
Sister, mother
And spirit of the river, spirit of the sea,
Suffer me not to be separated

And let my cry come unto Thee.

The prayer conveys acceptance of even elements of estrangement, the rocks image, in the light of acceptance of divine will. The importance of relationship to "His will" is signified in the petition "Suffer me not to be separated."

This last part of the *Ash Wednesday* sequence fuses the themes of the preceding sections and contributes to unifying them in one poem. The motif of life through death may be viewed on different planes. The penitent's struggle in the process of purgation, the tension between life and death of the self, the polarity of the natural and the divine, depict the conditions of estrangement, and stages toward reconciliation. In contrast to Eliot's earlier writings, the reality of a divine will is intrinsic in the poem, and the validity of submission to that will is basic in the thought development. Ambiguous though the imagery may be, and ambivalent though the penitent may appear, there is, nevertheless, the pervading theme of attraction toward God.

Introduction to Four Quartets

We have been tracing Eliot's quest from the waste land of meaninglessness, through the search for meaning in penance and purgation, and now are ready to continue the quest in new planes of experience. Considered by many as Eliot's most profound and significant work, *Four Quartets* explores man's meaning in relation to time. As the title suggests, the poem is structured in a pattern of musical form. The parallel use of point and counterpoint as sound and thought sustains the musical format. We are made aware of the contrasts between stillness and movement, past and present, beginning and end.

"Burnt Norton," the first of the quartets, is one of the most complex. In the opening section, the motifs of time and eternity, and reality and illusion are introduced. The first lines set forth the concepts of time.

> Time present and time past
> Are both perhaps present in the future,
> And time future contained in time past.
> If all time is eternally present
> All time is unredeemable.

The next lines consider memory and possibility in relation to the present, concluding that:

> What might have been and what has been
> Point to one end, which is always present.

The realm of possibility, of the other choice, is explored in the imagery of the passage not taken and the door never opened into the rose garden. Reflecting on the garden image, the protagonist continues in an illusory world, the world of vision through which he experiences a moment of reality.

> Other echoes
> Inhabit the garden. Shall we follow?
> Quick, said the bird, find them, find them,
> Round the corner. Through the first gate,
> Into our first world, shall we follow
> The deception of the thrush? Into our first world.
> There they were, dignified, invisible,
> Moving without pressure, over the dead leaves,
> In the autumn heat, through the vibrant air,
> And the bird called, in response to
> The unheard music hidden in the shrubbery,
> And the unseen eyebeam crossed, for the roses
> Had the look of flowers being looked at.

The world of "the might-have-been" inhabited by the selves "that could-have-been" is pictured. The unreal, the phantasy, seems real as the scene is detailed with formal boxwood garden, pool, and sunlight. The section closes with

> ... human kind
> Cannot bear very much reality.
> Time past and time future
> What might have been and what has been
> Point to one end, which is always present.

The worlds of illusion and reality, time past and future, the realm of possibility and of memory, meet in the present moment, the now. When the "one end" is viewed as "time eternally present," or the eternal now, it is understood as the point of reality where meaning is given. This moment out of time, or beyond time, suggests the moment immediate to God. Although the familiar structures of time are collapsed, in the apprehension of the timeless moment the meaning of time may be discovered. In this concept there is fulfillment of all the potential.

The second section of "Burnt Norton" opens with breaking down sense imagery rather than with collapsing time patterns.

Garlic and sapphires in the mud
Clot the bedded axle-tree.
The trilling wire in the blood
Sings below inveterate scars
And reconciles forgotten wars.
The dance along the artery
The circulation of the lymph
Are figured in the drift of stars
Ascend to summer in the tree
We move above the moving tree
In light upon the figured leaf
And hear upon the sodden floor
Below, the boarhound and the boar
Pursue their patterns as before
But reconciled among the stars.

The disparate images are all a part of a pattern of movement. Contrasts as extreme as the "circulation of the lymph" and the "drift of stars" are resolved in an eternal moving pattern. As we attempt to visualize the scene, we feel that psychedelic designs are thrust before us. Flux permeates the section as opposites are described in motion and are reconciled only in more encompassing patterns of natural forces.

The lines following the opening lyric contrast "the still point" with the movement of the introductory portion. Through negation and paradox, a definition of the still point is attempted. The final line offers a solution to the question of time by indicating the merger of the world of time with the eternal.

The third section of "Burnt Norton" begins with subway imagery providing a sense of time and motion. However, the dim light of the tube gives no suggestion of the light of "the still point," nor does the darkness of the "dark night of the soul." The subway riders are characterized in a manner reminiscent of earlier descriptions of meaningless and estranged existence. Here, in the "strained time-ridden faces" is no indication that time may be conquered through time.

The last part of this section moves from the meaningless underground of subway existence to meaningful depths of the way of purgation. The internal darkness of negation of the physical sphere and of the worlds of sense, phantasy, and spirit is one way to the end, to meaning. The other way is that of immediate apprehension, the moment of illumination. Here is Heraclitus' "the way up and the way down are one and the same." In contrast to the way of meaning, the world of our mechanized age moves

> In appetency, on its metalled ways
> Of time past and time future.

The brief fourth movement returns to the garden vision. Now, however, a twilight atmosphere pervades the scene and the "sun-loving" flowers are countered with the yew.

The fifth section of "Burnt Norton" considers the union of movement and stillness in the arts and relates it to the worlds of time and the still point. Words and music move only in time and so are limited by death. They can achieve "the stillness," the unchanging state, only by form or pattern. The pattern of movement and form, whether in arts of time such as music, or space like pottery, are paralleled in life in that

> . . . the end precedes the beginning,
> And the end and the beginning were always there
> Before the beginning and after the end.
> And all is always now. . . .

The next lines concentrate on the problem of utterance and move from difficulties of words to attack upon the Word. With the phrase "The Word in the desert," there is the first direct reference to the Incarnation, although the concept underlines the poem as a whole.

The final lines recapitulate the themes of the previous sections. Reference to "the figure of the ten stairs" of St. John of the Cross implies a pattern of discipline in attaining the timeless reality. The still point is acknowledged as love, and love as cause and end of movement is God.

> Love is itself unmoving,
> Only the cause and end of movement,
> Timeless, and undesiring
> Except in the aspect of time
> Caught in the form of limitation
> Between un-being and being.

"East Coker," the second poem in the sequence, reflects Eliot's consideration of man and history as he is confronted by the Second World War. The title comes from the tiny Somerset village of Eliot's ancestors, the reputed home of Sir Thomas Elyot, author of *The Book Named the Governour*, a work quoted in the first section of "East Coker." The opening line provides a key to the themes of the entire poem: "In my beginning is my end. . . ." Beginnings and patterns of time and history are to be explored. The first strophe stresses the cycle of life as illustrated in the successive rise of families and communities. The concluding lines of this first section continue the search for beginning, and through beginnings for identity.

> Dawn points, and another day
> Prepares for heat and silence. Out at sea the dawn wind
> Wrinkles and slides. I am here
> Or there, or elsewhere. In my beginning.

Here is silence, but not stillness. In the cycles and movement of this section there is no evidence of the still point.

The second movement of "East Coker" opens with confusion and broken patterns. Through unnatural seasonal associations, chaos, strife, and destruction of war are symbolized. There is disillusionment when the past is considered as a source of wisdom, and the conclusion declares:

> . . . Do not let me hear
> Of the wisdom of old men, but rather of their folly,
> Their fear of fear and frenzy, their fear of possession,
> Of belonging to another, or to others, or to God.
> The only wisdom we can hope to acquire
> Is the wisdom of humility: humility is endless.

The third movement details imagery of estrangement. Darkness pervades, and there is no pattern of movement. Here "vacant interstellar spaces" replace the pattern "reconciled among the stars" of "Burnt Norton." Darkness, vacuity, loss of sense and motivation characterize the age. Although there is activity, there is no goal for action. Although men know their profession, they know not their identity. Thus,

. . . we all go with them, into the silent funeral,
Nobody's funeral, for there is no one to bury.

Confronted with the overwhelming darkness, the protagonist turns
to transcendent darkness, to the darkness of God. By way of mystical paradox, death and rebirth are approached:

So the darkness shall be the light, and the stillness the
dancing.

Whisper of running streams, and winter lightning.
The wild thyme unseen and the wild strawberry,
The laughter in the garden, echoed ecstasy
Not lost, but requiring, pointing to the agony
Of death and birth.

The last portion of this movement reinforces the mystical theme
through the purgatorial way of St. John of the Cross. As in *Ash
Wednesday*, the way of negation, of total self-denial, becomes the
way of fulfillment.

To arrive where you are, to get from where you are not,
You must go by a way wherein there is no ecstasy.
In order to arrive at what you do not know
You must go by a way which is the way of ignorance.
In order to possess what you do not possess
You must go by the way of dispossession.
In order to arrive at what you are not
You must go through the way in which you are not.
And what you do not know is the only thing you know
And what you own is what you do not own
And where you are is where you are not.

The darkness and renunciation of the third movement are followed
by the figure of Christ the healer in the fourth movement. In
characterizing the surgeon as himself wounded, the poem alludes
to Christ's passion, wherein "he was wounded for our transgres-
sions . . . and with his stripes we are healed." Here is total and
ultimate renunciation.

We see in the hospital metaphor the spiritual sickness of the
world. Man's condition, under Adam's curse, is tainted by original
sin and can be cured only through first recognizing and acknowl-

edging the "disease." In brokenness and sickness, estrangement is suggested, and in return to wholeness reconciliation is implied.

The Eucharistic imagery and allusion to Good Friday in the last stanza climaxes the redemptive theme of this movement.

> The dripping blood our only drink,
> The bloody flesh our only food:
> In spite of which we like to think
> That we are sound, substantial flesh and blood—
> Again, in spite of that, we call this Friday good.

The final movement of "East Coker" opens with a personal self-inventory. Reflecting the consideration of the word as explored in "Burnt Norton," the poet re-examines his problem of expression and concludes that there must ever be struggle in "trying to learn to use words" and that "For us, there is only the trying. The rest is not our business."

The movement returns to the theme of time, of beginnings and ends, of memory and history.

> Home is where one starts from. As we grow older
> The world becomes stranger, the pattern more complicated
> Of dead and living. Not the intense moment
> Isolated, with no before and after,
> But a lifetime burning in every moment
> And not the lifetime of one man only
> But of old stones that cannot be deciphered.

As he considers the gifts of age, the poet observes

> Love is most nearly itself
> When here and now cease to matter.

This may not be "the intense moment, isolated" but it suggests that when time is transcended, absolute love may be known. Closely associated with "the still point," this experience of time transcended moves to place transcended. As the final lines declare,

> Old men ought to be explorers
> Here and there does not matter
> We must be still and still moving
> Into another intensity

For a further union, a deeper communion
Through the dark cold and the empty desolation,
The wave cry, the wind cry, the vast waters
Of the petrel and the porpoise. In my end is my beginning.

The vast waters of the closing lines of "East Coker" become a focal image in "The Dry Salvages," the third poem of *Four Quartets*. The symbols of river and sea predominate in exploring the rhythms of time and timelessness.

The landscape of Cape Ann with the off-shore rocks, the Dry Salvages, is the setting for consideration of the "river of life" as related to the "sea of time." In Eliot's words, "The river is within us, the sea is all about us." As he develops this first section, the river represents man's life from birth to death, and is a "reminder of what men choose to forget," their bondage to nature, their primitivism. In contrast, the sea symbolizes boundless time. The two concepts of time are reflected in the closing lines of the first movement.

In the description of the ground swell, the affirmations of the *Gloria Patri* re-echo, and control the bell which "sounds a warning and a summons," symbolic of death.

The second movement continues the mood of the "tolling bell" of death, picturing lifelessness or the death-in-life existence, devoid of purpose, and leading eventually to futile old age and death. The cyclic life of the fishermen, their endless rounds of sailing from and returning to port reinforces the theme. We see, too, the question of destination is interwoven throughout the section, but only in the reference to the Annunciation do we see a positive answer to the question of ends, of death.

In the allusion to the Annunciation, the pervasive theme of death is countered by the promise of birth. The poet again attempts to discern pattern and meaning in the past. Theories of time as sequence and as development are discarded. However, the past remains in memory and in "the eternal now," the simultaneity of time. The moment, the sudden illumination, is re-examined; with the conclusion that

We had the experience but missed the meaning,
And approach to the meaning restores the experience
In a different form, . . .

We are reminded that both moments of happiness and of agony remain, for "time the destroyer is time the preserver." Building on the image of the river as carrying wastage from the past, the poet alludes to "the bitter apple and the bite in the apple" to suggest the continuing presence of sin. However, in the "ragged rock" of the concluding lines he implies that there is also continuance of "perfected meaning" and "eternal stability."

> And the ragged rock in the restless waters,
> Waves wash over it, fogs conceal it;
> On a halycon day it is merely a monument,
> In navigable weather it is always a seamark
> To lay a course by: but in the sombre season
> Or the sudden fury, is what it always was.

Part three of "Dry Salvages" begins in a discursive mood, with the protagonist reiterating the themes of simultaneity of time and unity of opposites. Another aspect of time is considered in the thought of the changing person, precluding any return to the past or arrival at a known future. Quoting Krishna's teaching in the *Bhagavad-Gita*, the poet stresses the present moment as the only reality, and detachment from the self and its future as the means to another sphere of existence. Thus, Eliot interprets the Hindu teaching, not as a sequence of definite incarnations, but as the experience of rebirth in the present moment.

The short fourth movement turns again to the Lady and salutes her as guardian of all who are at sea. In the light of preceding sections, those who are at sea may imply all who are sojourners in time, and those "setting forth and not returning" may be a reminder that we never return the same persons as at our departure.

The final movement of "Dry Salvages" begins with a consideration of men's attitudes toward time. Astrology, fortune-telling, superstitious omens, and even psychoanalysis are cited as popular ways of interpreting the past and future. By contrast, only the saint is able "to apprehend/ The point of intersection of the timeless/ With time." We see that for the saint this is,

> . . . something given
> And taken, in a lifetime's death in love,
> Ardour and selflessness and self-surrender.
> For most of us, there is only the unattended
> Moment, the moment in and out of time,

These moments of illumination, described in "Burnt Norton," are declared to be "only hints and guesses," while

> ... the rest
> Is prayer, observance, discipline, thought and action.
> The hint half guessed, the gift half understood, is Incarnation.
> Here the impossible union.
> Of spheres of existence is actual,
> Here the past and future
> Are conquered, and reconciled,

In these lines we see all the themes of preceding sections. In the Incarnation all time is reconciled, the eternal and temporal spheres of existence are actualized in one reality, and the moments of illumination are fulfilled. This focal point of the poem is followed by an affirmation that life may have purpose and meaning even if it is devoid of ecstasy.

> ... And right action is freedom
> From past and future also.
> For most of us, this is the aim
> Never here to be realised;
> Who are only undefeated
> Because we have gone on trying;
> We, content at last
> If our temporal reversion nourish
> (Not too far from the yew-tree)
> The life of significant soil.

Perhaps, in the reference to the yew tree, rebirth as well as death is symbolized and acceptance of the completion of life provides a sense of significance.

"Little Gidding," the concluding sequence of *Four Quartets,* like the preceding poems, has a definite geographical and historical setting. In the early seventeenth century, Nicholas Ferrar founded in this Huntingdonshire village a spiritual community which became famous for its piety. The allusion to coming "at night like a broken king" refers to King Charles's allegedly finding shelter there after his defeat at Naseby. Thus, it is in an atmosphere of piety, prayer, and even defeat that Eliot continues his consideration of time and eternity, appearance and reality, sin and grace.

The first movement opens with apprehension of meaning in the unseasonal spring day of mid-winter. As he frequently does, Eliot uses the particular experience to suggest a universal, "the eternal brightness of God," or the promise of the Divine Summer beyond time. The unexpected moment of illumination is suggestive of another sphere of illuminating experience, Pentecost.

When the short day is brightest, with frost and fire,
The brief sun flames the ice, on pond and ditches,
In windless cold that is heart's heat,
Reflecting in a watery mirror
A glare that is blindness in the early afternoon.
And glow more intense than blaze of branch or brazier,
Stirs the dumb spirit: no wind, but pentecostal fire
In the dark time of the year. . . .

The wonder of the unexpected which pervades the first part of the movement gives way to consideration of plan and purpose in the next portion. The approach to the chapel of Little Gidding, no matter what the time or season, is seen to be an approach to fulfill-ment.

. . . And what you thought you came for
Is only a shell, a husk of meaning
From which the purpose breaks only when it is fulfilled
If at all. Either you had no purpose
Or the purpose is beyond the end you figured
And is altered in fulfilment. . . .

In the last part of this movement, the poet concludes,

. . . You are here to kneel
Where prayer has been valid. And prayer is more
Than an order of words, the conscious occupation
Of the praying mind, or the sound of the voice praying.
And what the dead had no speech for, when living,
They can tell you, being dead: the communication
Of the dead is tongued with fire beyond the language of
    the living.
Here, the intersection of the timeless moment
Is England and nowhere. Never and always.

The Wasteland, Ash Wednesday, Four Quartets   115

Here again, past and present are brought together, meeting in eternity; and eternity, incorporating all time and place, is yet placeless and timeless.

The second movement begins with a mood of destruction and hopelessness as reflecting the war years in which it was written. The death of the elements (air, earth, water, and fire) signifies total destruction. Desolation with no sign of renewal pervades. Against this setting of total disintegration, an episode reflecting Eliot's nights on London fire patrol is recounted. In the moment between the departure of the last bomber and the sounding of the "all clear" of the air raid, the poet encounters "a familiar compound ghost." The composite figures of Eliot's poetic teachers is viewed in detachment by the poet who has "assumed a double part," reporting,

> Too strange to each other for misunderstanding,
> In concord at this intersection time
> Of meeting nowhere, no before and after,
> We trod the pavement in a dead patrol.

For the "ghost," the transition from death to the desolation and death of war seems to be easy, since

> . . . the passage now presents no hindrance
> To the spirit unappeased and peregrine
> Between two worlds become much like each other,

Acknowledging a mutual interest in words and speech, the ghost warns that age promises no success but only weakness, disappointment, and disillusion. The most trying gift of age is

> . . . the rending pain of re-enactment
> Of all that you have done, and been; the shame
> Of motives late revealed, and the awareness
> Of things ill done and done to others' harm
> Which once you took for exercise of virtue.
> Then fools' approval stings, and honour stains.
> From wrong to wrong the exasperated spirit
> Proceeds, unless restored by that refining fire
> Where you must move in measure, like a dancer.

The sense of destruction and brokenness of war appears as another "waste land" of estranged man. In the allusion to refining fire, the purgatorial way to restoration is indicated, and in the dance, a symbol of reconciliation (the still point) may be suggested.

The third movement opens in a discursive mood, with the consideration of two aspects of love, attachment and detachment. The change from attachment to self to detachment from self, to uncalculating love, seems to be natural, "Occurring in the proper course of things." In detachment, personal love is not lost in indifference, but is absorbed in something larger.

> . . . See, now they vanish,
> The faces and places, with the self which, as it could, loved
>   them,
> To become renowned, transfigured, in another pattern.

The movement changes with the quotation from Dame Julian of Norwich.

> Sin is Behovely, but
> All shall be well, and
> All manner of thing shall be well.

Although sin is inescapable, inevitable, Dame Julian discovers that it can bring humility and discipline leading men to greater knowledge of divine love. Thus, in the mood of "All manner of thing shall be well," the protagonist looks back through history, on warring factions, victors and victims, ancient policies, and concludes:

> Whatever we inherit from the fortunate
> We have taken from the defeated
> What they had to leave us—a symbol:
> A symbol perfected in death.
> And all shall be well and
> All manner of thing shall be well
> By the purification of the motive
> In the ground of our beseeching.

According to Dame Julian, "the ground of our beseeching" is Love; therefore "the motive force in this spiritual strife is love."

The lyric fourth movement opens with imagery of fire on different levels of correspondence. Pentecostal tongues of fire, purgatorial flames, and the fires of war are all present in the first stanza.

> The dove descending breaks the air
> With flame of incandescent terror
> Of which the tongues declare
> The one discharge from sin and error.
> The only hope, or else despair
>   Lies in the choice of pyre or pyre—
>   To be redeemed from fire by fire.

The second stanza continues the theme of choice between the fire of self-love and the fire of the love of God. The choice is inevitable, but man may be consumed by fires of destruction or renewed by the redeeming fire of God.

The final movement consummates not only "Little Gidding," but the entire *Four Quartets*. The earlier themes are reviewed and resolved. The death and rebirth motif is reflected in the opening lines on beginnings and ends.

> What we call the beginning is often the end
> And to make an end is to make a beginning.
> The end is where we start from. . . .

Following this, the poet reconsiders the struggle with words which is a necessary part of poetic art, and concludes that here, too, "Every phrase and every sentence is an end and a beginning,/ Every poem an epitaph." In action, the same principle holds true, wherefore,

> We die with the dying:
> See, they depart, and we go with them.
> We are born with the dead:
> See, they return, and bring us with them.
> The moment of the rose, and the moment of the yew-tree
> Are of equal duration. . . .

From this statement of simultaneity of life and death, the poet develops a reappraisal of the problem of redeeming time, noting that

> . . . A people without history
> Is not redeemed from time, for history is a pattern
> Of timeless moments. . . .

Furthermore, he makes clear to us the existence and actuality of time at Little Gidding.

> . . . So, while the light fails
> On a winter's afternoon, in a secluded chapel
> History is now and England.

The first half of this final movement returns to Julian of Norwich in "with the drawing of this Love and the voice of this Calling." Here, in love, is the ground of life and death, end and beginning, creature and creation, time and eternity.

The final strophe admits

> We shall not cease from exploration
> And the end of all our exploring
> Will be to arrive where we started
> And know the place for the first time.

Reviewing the earlier moments of illumination and the imagery of meaning, the protagonist discovers that their apprehension requires

> A condition of complete simplicity
> (Costing not less than everything)

As a result,

> . . . all shall be well and
> All manner of thing shall be well
> When the tongues of flame are in-folded
> Into the crowned knot of fire
> And the fire and the rose are one.

In this finale, the antitheses and paradoxes of all the preceding lines are resolved. In the "flame . . . in-folded/Into the crowned knot of fire" conquering Love reconciles the imagery of estrangement and restoration, destruction and fulfillment, making of them "one."

Viewed as a whole, *Four Quartets* provides rich ground for exploring the meaning of man's life in the world of time. In the imagery and discourses on different spheres of existence, the goal of man is portrayed as final restoration to the "ground of his being," or to the first cause, Love. Although physical cycles of life and death recur in different figures and patterns, fulfillment is never indicated on this plane, but rather is promised in the moments of illumination and transcendence.

Although the epiphanies and annunciations are charged with momentary fulfillment, the ultimate restoration of man is indicated as grounded on "the drawing of this Love and the voice of this Calling."

In our sojourn with Eliot, we have traversed the waste land of meaningless existence, where desolation and barrenness pervade the landscape. Turning from the sterility of *The Waste Land*, we have sought for a way of renewal and of meaning in *Ash Wednesday*. Through humility and penitence, we have been granted moments of illumination and an assurance that meaning can be discovered in our existence. Although *Ash Wednesday* provides promise of personal renewal, it leaves us pondering the basic questions of relationships in the larger spheres of time and place. *Four Quartets* moves us beyond the personal to the universal, while keeping us mindful of our individual relationships to history and the vastness of interstellar space. We confront the question of purpose and see it in the perspective of divine order. Time in relation to the timeless and place in relation to the universal spheres stretch our minds and spirits. Questions remain unanswered, but the sense of the undergirding law of love, the ground of our being, allows acceptance of the all life, including the questions. As individuals, we sense the beginning and end of our existence to be bound to this law of love, made manifest in history in the Incarnate Word. Thus, to follow Eliot's quest requires us to see ourselves and our world in the perspective both of time and the timeless, of place and the spheres beyond our charting, and to know that the timeless has entered time and granted to place its significance.

The Last Gentleman

An Introduction and Commentary

WALKER PERCY has said of the hero of his second novel, *The Last Gentleman:* "He is what Gabriel Marcel calls a wayfarer—like an old-fashioned pilgrim on a serious quest."[1] And again, with reference to the same book: "The lostness of the American in America is a paradigm of the existentialist or even the Christian view."[2] With these statements he establishes his religious and philosophical preoccupations, not only in *The Last Gentleman* but also in his equally interesting, if less accomplished, first novel, *The Moviegoer.*

One may easily be dazzled by the surface brilliance, the splendid language, and the successful comic and ironic effects in these books (and it is true that Dr. Percy deliberately maintains a certain tone and pace—a *surface*—in order to mask his deepest concerns, not because he is afraid to state them, but because he is convinced that it is impossible to state them except tangentially and comically); but in order to read these books intelligently, one must set aside for the moment one's delight in the writer's mastery of craft and keep before him instead the ideas of man as a wayfarer and of the lostness of the American in America as points to which every scene and effect can be referred.

I should also say here, with regard to method, that in every case I have used Dr. Percy's own words, that is, the context of the book, to elucidate its meaning. *The Last Gentleman* means what it says; and it speaks with great clarity if one takes the trouble to read carefully. It touches upon a great many other subjects and themes than those illustrated by the words I have chosen to quote (I have scarcely considered, for example, its aspect as social satire), but the text is available and will reward the reader's close attention.

About the Author

The life which brought Walker Percy to the writing of these two highly original novels and to the philosophical, psychiatric, and linguistic inquiries that have been appearing over the past ten years in such magazines as *The Sewanee Review, Commonweal, America,* and *The Partisan Review* began in Birmingham, Alabama, in 1916. Here he lived with his parents until the death, first, of his father by suicide, and shortly thereafter, of his mother in an automobile accident. After these two tragedies, Percy came, with his brothers, to live with his father's first cousin, William Alexander Percy, in Greenville, Mississippi. At that time he was fourteen years old.

Since *The Last Gentleman* has as an integral part of its structure and theme the superimposition of the lives of grandfather, father, and son, one upon another in the mind of the antagonist; and since the background and characters in the novel are borne upon by the background and characters of the Percy family, it is relevant to go very briefly into the family history.

The critic is fortunate to have an exhaustive firsthand account of this history in the form of an autobiography, *Lanterns on the Levee,* by William Alexander Percy, who was a minor poet and lawyer in the Mississippi Delta in the nineteen-twenties and thirties. Here one learns that the family settled in Mississippi early in the nineteenth century; that they were, from their earliest years in this raw and unfortunate land, committed to an active part in its political and moral life; and that this commitment extended not only to the state and to the South but, wherever it was possible to put strength and wealth and intelligence and influence to use, to the nation.

William Alexander Percy's grandfather, a strong Whig and anti-secessionist before the Civil War, nonetheless (like Lee and others who were opposed both to slavery and to secession) raised a company and fought with the South throughout the war. Afterward, during the Reconstruction, he was a leader of the fight for white supremacy in the Mississippi Delta and was known to his contemporaries as the "Gray Eagle of the Delta." "In those days," W. A. Percy writes, "you had to be a hero or a villain or a weakling—you couldn't be just middling ordinary."[3] Clearly he believed his grandfather to be a hero.

LeRoy Percy, the son of the "Gray Eagle," fought the Populist (and racist) regime of Vardaman and was briefly United States Senator from Mississippi. His brother, Walker, (the present Walker Percy's grandfather) went over to Mississippi from his home in Alabama to help in the campaign for re-election, which, after a bitter and vituperative struggle, resulted in Percy's overwhelming defeat.

William Alexander Percy, although his bent was literary, was a practicing lawyer and a successful planter like his father. He was one of the leaders of the fight against the Ku Klux Klan in the nineteen-twenties and, with other moderates, helped to create the atmosphere of genuine (if somewhat sluggish and self-satisfied) racial and political moderation that has made Greenville an anomaly in the racist climate of Mississippi in the nineteen-fifties and sixties.

These men (Walker Percy's grandparents, great-uncle, and the cousin who was a father to him during his boyhood) and other men like them, educated in the East, deeply conservative, "honorable" by the curiously anachronistic standards of the feudal South, were what people used to call "gentlemen." They practiced, according to the last of them, the Stoicism of Marcus Aurelius with a leavening of Episcopal frivolity and a ballast of Presbyterian Calvinism. Although to many students of the Reconstruction period, it appears that the earliest of these post-Civil War Southerners, the first Bourbons, by their use of racism in the fight against the Populist movement, scuttled the feeble beginnings of a viable biracial political system in the south, it may be true that they did represent, as W. A. Percy believed they did, the best of the nineteenth-century South—flawed though it was at best. And they watched what they believed to be a good world crumble and fall into ruins before the political power of the common man and the vulgar mass industrialism of the twentieth century.

Like a great many Southern families who have roots in Mississippi and Louisiana, the Percy clan married into the Creole society of New Orleans and drew into itself the influence of Catholicism. Walker Percy's other set of great-grandparents were French Catholics, and Catholicism has been toyed with or embraced by various members of the family.

Here, then, in the world from which Walker Percy comes, we have two areas of commitment, two ways by which men have lived their lives: the Stoa, in its peculiarly Protestant-touched, violent, Southern form, and Catholicism. The third and newest area, in which all men in the twentieth century are forced to live, is the modern world—a world in which a man like Percy may find himself at home neither in any church nor in the swashbuckling, aristocratic humanism of his fathers. Indeed, he is at home nowhere. The Southern Stoa has been not only defeated but discredited as a viable way of life in the twentieth century. Nor can he be moved by the "socially oriented" church, the Rotary Club religion that so often passes for Christianity these days. He is a pilgrim. He has come *from;* he is going *toward.* But he does not know toward what.

In Walker Percy's case, these dilemmas are intensified and made poignant by the thread of suicide in the family. In generation after generation, from the first Percy who settled at Woodville, Mississippi, toward the end of the eighteenth century, through the ancestor who killed himself in grief after his daughter's death, down to Walker Percy's father, they have heard and resisted with more difficulty than most men the sweet voice of death. Or perhaps it is simply that they are men to whom choices are immediate. They must make them or die. They *cannot* live comfortably in the world.

Also, in his case (and it seems as if God must have put his hand on this writer and formed him specifically for his own purposes by making available to him certain peculiarly relevant areas of human experience), Percy was removed from the world of action and decision, in which his family had always functioned, and turned in upon himself with the greatest intensity during his early manhood. He graduated with high honors from Columbia University's College of Physicians and Surgeons in 1941, and, the following year, during his internship at Bellevue Hospital, where, as he has written, "I did all the autopsies on TB deaths, sans mask or gloves," he contracted tuberculosis. He was an invalid at Saranac Lake, New York, for two years. There he lived "first in an attic room of a boarding house for some months and saw nobody but a maid who brought me a tray of food . . . and then in Trudeau Sanitorium, where I knew Larry Doyle, a famous infielder for the New York Giants."

Thus Percy submitted himself first to the rigorous intellectual discipline of science and then, perforce, to the equally rigorous discipline of invalidism.

It was at Saranac Lake that he began to read the existentialists:

Dostoevsky's *Notes from Underground,* then Kierkegaard, some of whose works were being translated at that time, and later Heidegger, Gabriel Marcel, Sartre, and Camus. He says of himself, "So I began to be interested in other things besides science. My devotion to science is still with me—I like its elegance and precision. It is simply that I became aware of some of its shortcomings, and Kierkegaard helped me to see them. He said, 'Hegel told everything about the world except one thing; what it is to be a man and to live and to die.' "[4]

After his bout with tuberculosis, he returned slowly, impeded by intermittent periods of illness, to the world. In 1946 he was married. In 1947 he was converted to Catholicism. He did not resume the practice of medicine, but moved to Covington, Louisiana, and began to write. Here, with his wife and two daughters, he continues to live.

Introduction to the Book

The characters in *The Last Gentleman,* thrown by the most tenuous chance into intimacy with one another are these: Williston Bibb Barrett—Will—a young bachelor from the Mississippi Delta— the last of a line of "honorable men"; Kitty Vaught, a girl whom Will happens to see through his telescope when he is in Central Park watching birds and buildings; and her family—Poppy Vaught, a wealthy Southerner, owner of a Chevrolet agency in a city like Atlanta or Birmingham; Mrs. Vaught, a genial and aristocratic Southern matron who believes that the Russians are conspiring to murder us all by fluoridating our water systems; Sutter Vaught, the elder son, a failed doctor who, according to his family, is interested in almost nothing but sex; Sutter's ex-wife, Rita, in whose attachment to Kitty overtones of homosexuality are evident; Val Vaught, the elder daughter, who has been converted to Catholicism and is a nun working with retarded Negro children in Georgia, and Jamie Vaught, the brilliant and delightful younger son who at sixteen is dying of leukemia.

The framework within which these very concretely realized characters operate is a relatively simple one. The opening of the book finds Will Barrett working as a "humidification engineer"—a kind of glorified nightwatchman, his night hours spent deep in the bowels of Macy's basement at the control board of the building's heating system. By day he sleeps at the YMCA. Will Barrett knows that there is something very wrong with himself:

> There were times when he was as normal as anybody. . . . [But] to be specific, he had now a nervous condition and suffered spells of amnesia. . . . Much of the time he was like a man who has just crawled out of a bombed building. Everything looked strange. Such a predicament, however, is not altogether a bad thing. Like the sole survivor of a bombed building, he had no secondhand opinions and he could see things afresh. (p. 17, *passim*)

He has tried analysis, but he is quite literally unable to reveal himself to his analyst and, although he is polite and agreeable during his hours on the couch, finds that he is able to "con" the doctor into believing almost anything he cares to say about himself.

In the opening scenes of the book, Dr. Percy establishes a strong sense of the ingratiating, and at the same time sentient, character of Will Barrett and also evokes the presence of the city as a desert and of the world as a terrifyingly solid and inescapable presence. He sets Barrett in this "moraine," this "roaring twilight" where the air is "thick as mustard gas" with "the sad noxious particles that befoul the sorrowful old Eastern sky," and where the city is "all solid and sullen from being the same today as yesterday," and then he has him break off his analysis and spend almost the last of his money to buy a telescope. By these strange measures, the meaning of which Will Barrett truly does not know, perhaps he will learn something that will enable him to live in the world.

"Often nowadays," Dr. Percy writes, "people live out their lives as if they were waiting for some sign or other. This young man was such a person."

And, with regard to the telescope:

> He focused on a building clear across the park. . . . There sprang into view a disc of brickwork perhaps eight feet in diameter. . . . He drew up a chair, . . . and gazed another five minutes at the bricks. He slapped his leg. It was as he had hoped. Not only were the bricks seen as if they were ten feet away; they were better than that. It was better than having the bricks there before him. They gained in value. Every grain and crack and excrescence became available. Beyond any doubt, he said to himself, this proves that bricks, as well as other things, are not as accessible as they used to be. Special measures are needed to recover them.
> The telescope recovered them. (p. 32)

The sign for which Will is waiting is the sight of Kitty Vaught.

. . . until this moment [the moment of seeing Kitty] he had lived in a state of pure possibility, not knowing what sort of a man he was or what he must do, and supposing therefore that he must be all men and do everything. But after this morning's incident his life took a turn in a particular direction. Thereafter he came to see that he was not destined to do everything but only one or two things. (pp. 11-12)

He falls in love with Kitty (at first sight), contrives a meeting with her, and thereafter knows that the one thing he must do is to follow her. He consents wholeheartedly, though bewilderedly, to being drawn into the complex life of her family. To the members of the family, he becomes the very person who can encourage, entertain, and be a companion to their dying son, Jamie. He agrees to do this, and he quits his job at Macy's and joins Jamie, during a brief remission from the disease, in a trip down the Atlantic Coast to the family home.

After a short stay with the Vaughts, during which he becomes a friend to the dying boy, acquainted with the other members of the family, and engaged to Kitty, he sets out to follow Sutter Vaught, who, for reasons of his own, has decided to take Jamie to New Mexico to die. During these two journeys, southward from New York and westward to New Mexico, Will Barrett has a series of lunatic adventures and encounters with the denizens of the modern wilderness. He finds Jamie in a hospital in Santa Fe, and there he waits, does what he can for the boy, and watches him die.

Early in the book, Dr. Percy has said of Will, "He was an unusual young man. But perhaps nowadays it is not so unusual. What distinguished him anyhow was this: he had to know everything before he could do anything" (p. 11). At the end, Will is still trying to know everything in order to act; but the possibility is raised that, although he is not yet fully conscious of it, action may now be possible to him.

The people who move in and out of this story, and who are set in the real and fully imagined world of Will Barrett's pilgrimage, may be said to illustrate in their various ways the choices that are open to Barrett and the nature of the world in which he must make these choices. But this is true in a novelistic, rather than a didactic, sense. *First* these people are alive, acting out their own fates in ways that seem wholly inevitable.

The group of characters that comprise Barrett's own family, what he comes *from*, are presented in a broken series of recollections and background passages that occur throughout the book and that may present some difficulty to the reader. The author makes it clear that Will Barrett, in his state of dislocation, is sometimes not at all sure who he is. (During his periods of amnesia, or "fugue," for example, he may wake up suddenly to find himself wandering through a Civil War battlefield in northern Virginia or working for "three months for a florist in Cincinnati, assaulted by the tremendous *déjà vus* of hot green growing things," and with no idea how he has come to be there.) Barrett has become so thoroughly entangled in the lives of his parents and grandparents that even when he is functioning with apparent competence, he is often not entirely sure what has happened to him and what has happened to his father and to his grandfather. And sometimes the reader is not sure either. His knowledge of the smells and sounds and appearance of things in the nineteen twenties and thirties seems to be his own, and yet he was not born until 1939. Was he the boy who overheard a certain conversation between his father and Senator Oscar Underwood on the train, or was it his father who overheard his grandfather? Even with regard to the suicide of his father, the reader is not sure unless he reads very carefully that the man who killed himself was Will's father and that "the boy" who was present was Will. By this device (and once one has examined it, it seems a particularly felicitous one), Dr. Percy makes very real indeed the profound influence of family life that has been the theme of so many Southern writers. In truth, we *are* our parents and our grandparents in the very way that Will Barrett is his father and his grandfather. One of the two epigraphs that Dr. Percy has chosen for his book is from Kierkegaard's *Either/Or:* "If a man cannot forget, he will never amount to much." From this we can only conclude that a part of Will Barrett's pilgrimage must be to leave forever behind him the seductive world of his own past.

And who are the men with whom this addled young fellow feels so profound and so crippling an identity? They are the representatives of the Stoa, of the flawed Southern tradition of *noblesse oblige*, of whom W. A. Percy writes in *Lanterns on the Levee.*

In this connection, it is interesting to note that various incidents and attitudes recounted in *Lanterns on the Levee* reappear in other forms in *The Last Gentleman*. For example, Will Barrett has taken up boxing at Princeton because his sense of honor would not let him take a "cut" from a snobbish New Englander; and he decides that if he is to protect his honor, he'd better be prepared to do so effectively. Walker Percy's attitude toward the incident is ironic, W. A. Percy's, when he tells the same story in *Lanterns on the Levee*, is literal.

Also apparent in the evaluation of the lives of Will's father and grandfathers is a haunting similarity to the words of W. A. Percy's lament for the end of his era:

The great grandfather [Walker Percy writes] knew what was what and said so and acted accordingly and did not care what anyone thought. . . . [The grandfather] was brave but he gave much thought to the business of being brave. He too would have shot it out with the Grand Wizard [of the KKK] if only he could have made certain it was the thing to do. (p. 16)

But the father:

More than anything else, he wished to act with honor and to be thought well of by other men. So living for him was a strain. He became ironical. For him it was not a small thing to walk down the street on an ordinary September morning. In the end he was killed by his own irony and sadness and by the strain of living out an ordinary day in a perfect dance of honor. (p. 16)

W. A. Percy wrote again and again of this same subject, although he did not write of it in the same way: ". . . we have lost the old ideals, the old strengths. . . ." "Honor and honesty, compassion and truth are good even if they kill you, for they alone give life it's dignity and worth . . ." and:

The old Southern way of life in which I had been reared existed no more and its values were ignored or derided. Negroes used to be servants, now they were problems; manners used to be a branch of morals, now they were merely bad; poverty used to be worn with style and dignity, now it was a stigma of failure; politics used to be the study of men proud and jealous of America's honor, now it was a game played by self-seekers which no man need bother his head about. Where there had been an accepted pattern of living, there was no pattern whatsoever.[5]

There, in these words, is the nineteenth-century South with all its true values and with all its terrible flaws.

In any case, Will Barrett, the last of the fictional line, a humidification engineer at Macy's,

> . . . did not know what to think. So he became a watcher and a listener and a wanderer. He could not get enough of watching. Once when he was a boy, a man next door had gone crazy and had sat out in his back yard pitching gravel around and hollering. . . . The boy watched him all day . . . his mouth open and drying. It seemed to him that if he could figure out what was wrong with the man he would learn the great secret of life. (p. 16)

Will never stops wondering why that man was hollering, and in the course of the book, we come back to him and to men like him again and again; but here I wish only to note that Will is beginning to know that his father's world is dead. Its only remnants are the widowed aunts who still live in Mississippi; and the old man, Uncle Fannin, whose residence in a broken-down family place in a ghost town that used to be a ferry landing (appropriately named Shut Off) indicates clearly enough the author's view of the present effectiveness of the Southern ethical man.

Then there are the members of the Vaught family, who present to Will various other ways of living in the world. Rita Vaught, Sutter's ex-wife, aside from being one of the most convincingly unattractive women in recent American literature, may be said to represent the modern, liberal, dilettantish, "unselfish" aesthete. Rita, who has been financing ballet lessons for Kitty in New York for more than a year (although there is never the faintest indication that Kitty could possibly become a successful ballet dancer) is the kind of woman who has a house in New Mexico and who gets "hung up" on Indian rituals. "Ree's been giving me the most fascinating account of the hikuli rite which is practiced by the Huichol Indians," Kitty says. "The women are absolved from their sins by tying knots in a palm-leaf string, one knot for each lover. Then they throw the string into Grandfather Fire" (pp. 87-88). Rita speaks of life and death in the most gruesomely playful and platitudinous way:

> "Our Jamie is not going to make it, Bill," she said in a low thrilling voice and with a sweetness that struck a pang to the marrow. . . .
> "So it's not such a big thing," she said softly. "One small adolescent as against the thirty thousand Japanese children we polished off."

"How's that?" said the engineer, cupping his good ear.

"At Hiroshima and Nagasaki."

"I don't, ah—"

"But this little guy happens to be a friend of mine. And yours.". . .

Oh, and I'm sick too, he thought anxiously, looking at his hands. Why is it that bad news is not so bad and good news not so good and what with the bad news being good, aye that is what makes her well and me sick? Oh, I'm not well. He was silent, gazing at his open hands on his knees.

. . . He saw that she was disappointed by his listlessness. She had wanted him to join her stand beside her and celebrate the awfulness. (pp. 79-80)

Another version of this same world view is represented by the "pseudo-Negro," the journalist who has dyed himself brown in order to travel through the South and find out the "real truth" about race relations. A platitudinous liberal like Rita, he succeeds, in a hilarious episode on the trip south, in getting Barrett punched in the nose by a woman from Haddon Heights, New Jersey, who mistakes the two of them for real estate "block breakers."

Once Will reaches the Vaught home, it is to Sutter Vaught that he attaches himself with real desperation. It seems to him that Sutter is the man who can answer his questions, can tell him why it is that he, Will, cannot live comfortably in the world—why he cannot simply "wed him a wife and live him a life"; why the air is full of noxious and ravening particles; why the bricks are so solid and full of themselves that one cannot see them; why, at the moments when he should feel all the acceptable emotions toward Kitty, he feels instead, discomfort, misery, and an overwhelming desire to run away; why he is happy in disaster and unable to support the misery of an ordinary Wednesday afternoon; why, when he suffers most from this enclosing world, he loses his memory and ceases to be able to function at all.

And it is true that Sutter understands far better than Will what is the matter, although it is not true that he has found any answers —or at least any answers that would be useful to Will. Sutter, in the philosophical scheme of *The Last Gentleman,* represents the failed scientist. He is a good doctor who first learned to transcend, to escape from, the enclosing world that Will cannot support, through the discipline of science, and then found that this transcendence did not solve the problem of how to be a man and to live and to die. He sought to re-enter the world of immediate reality, of immanence, through sex; and he writes the record of his efforts in the journal and casebook that he leaves (as if by accident) for Will to read during his trip to Mexico in search of Jamie (for Sutter is expecting Will to follow and to find them).

Sutter has already had conversations with Will in which he tries by hints and indirection to make him understand the nature of his predicament. For example, Sutter says:

"What is the meaning of this proverb: a stitch in time saves nine?"
"I would have to think about it and tell you later," said the engineer, a queer light in his eye. (p. 176)

(It is worth noting here that Percy refers to Will Barrett throughout the book as "the engineer," a title that is ludicrous except in the sense that, like every man, he is the engineer who is building his own life. And perhaps we should refer to "Doctor" Percy in the same sense: as a doctor who has long since ceased to practice the curing of bodies and is interested wholly in cures of another sort.)

But, to continue the conversation quoted above, Sutter says:

"You can't take time off to tell me now?"
"No."
"You really can't tell me, can you?"
"No."
"Why can't you?"
"You know why."
"You mean it is like asking a man hanging from a cliff to conjugate an irregular verb?"
"No. I'm not hanging from a cliff. It's not that bad. It's not that I'm afraid."
"What is it then?"
The engineer was silent.
"Is it rather that answering riddles does not seem important to you. Not as important as—" Sutter paused.
"As what?" asked the engineer, smiling.
"Isn't that for you to tell me?" (pp. 176-177)

In another conversation, equally oblique, Sutter tells Barrett of how, when he was practicing medicine, he was summoned to the home of a prominent businessman, a wealthy and cheerful fellow who had everything that the material world could give him but who was standing in the middle of his living room, dressed for work, holding his attaché case in his hand and screaming—screaming as Will had seen the neighbor of his boyhood stand in the middle of his yard and scream. Sutter's prescription for this type of disorder is to put the patient in the terminal ward of a hospital where he is surrounded by the dying. Here he quickly recovers his wits and becomes cheerful again. But Sutter will not answer Will's question: "Do you mean that in the terminal ward he discovered only that he was not so bad off, or is there more to it than that?"

And he will not or cannot answer Will's question: *What is the matter with me? What am I looking for?*

In Sutter's journals, there are more specific comments on the nature of human difficulties, comments that Will does not always understand but that he reads and ponders.

Lewdness = sole concrete metaphysic of layman in age of science = sacrament of the dispossessed. Things, persons, relations emptied out, not by theory, but by lay reading of theory. . . . Thus layman now believes that entire spectrum of relations between persons (e.g., a man and woman who seem to be connected by old complexus of relations, fondness, fidelity, and the like, understanding, the comic, etc. is based on "real" substratum of genital sex. . . . Pornography stands in a mutual relation to science and Christianity and is reinforced by both. (p. 221)

. . . The perfect pornographer = lapsed Christian Southerner (who as such retains the memory not merely of Christianity but of a region immersed in place and time) who presently in Berkeley or Ann Arbor, which are not true places but sites of abstract activity which could take place anywhere else, a map coordinate; who is perhaps employed as psychological tester or opinion sampler or other para-scientific pursuit." (p. 221)

[And again:] Man who falls victim to transcendence as the spirit of abstraction, i.e., elevates self against the world which is *pari passu* demoted to immanence and seen as exemplar and specimen and coordinate, and who is not at same time compensated by beauty of motion of method of science, has no choice but to seek reentry into immanent world *qua* immanence. But since no avenue of reentry remains save genital and since reentry coterminus c orgasm, post-orgasmic despair without remedy. Of my series of four suicides in scientists and technicians, 3 post-coital (spermatozoa at meatus) 2 in hotel room. Hotel room = site of intersection of transcendence and immanence: room itself, a triaxial coordinate ten floors above street; whore who comes up = pure immanence to be entered. But entry doesn't avail: one skids off into transcendence. *There is no reentry from the orbit of transcendence.* (p. 269)

Of himself he says, "I accept the current genital condition of all human relations and try to go beyond it. I cultivate pornography in order to set it at naught" (p. 271). And, "Watch a soap opera on TV where everyone is decent (and also sad, you will notice, as sad as lewdness is sad; I am the only American who is both lewd and merry). (p. 230)

But Sutter does not believe that he can help Barrett. He writes of him, "[He's got] a whiff of the transcendent trap and has got the wind up. But what can one tell him?" (p. 276)

Sutter does not even, in spite of all his understanding, have anything to tell himself. He has already attempted suicide once, and he is thinking again of killing himself. He has discarded religion as an answer to the "transcendent trap." And it must be that even "merry" pornography, "moral" pornography, does not work for him.

Nor does he believe that Val's answers are valid. In the journal and casebook, parts of which are addressed to her. He has considered her position as a practicing Catholic and rejected it:

I do not deny, Val, that a revival of your sacramental system is an alternative to lewdness (the only other alternative is the forgetting of the old sacrament), for lewdness itself is a kind of sacrament (devilish, if you like). The difference is that my sacrament is operational and yours is not. (p. 222)

Again: "The only difference between me and you is that you think that purity and life can only come from eating the body and drinking the blood of Christ. I don't know where it comes from" (p. 223).

As for Val's own account of her conversion, she tells Will Barrett of the nun, met by chance, who said, "What's the matter with you?" and "Come with me."

"That was it." [She said.] "I received instruction, . . . was shriven, baptized, confirmed, and made my first vows, all in the space of six weeks. The Bishop of Newark required that I get a statement from my doctor that there was no insanity in the family. When all I'd done was take them at their word."

And:

". . . I believe the whole business: God, the Jews, Christ, the Church, grace, and the forgiveness of sins—and . . . I'm meaner than ever. Christ is my Lord and I love him but I'm a good hater. . . . I still hope my enemies fry in hell. What to do about that? Will God forgive me?" (p. 236)

At the end of this conversation, Val takes the engineer's fumbling, embarrassed donation to her school for retarded Negro children and tells him good-bye. "I'll pray for you," she said absently. "Will you pray for me to receive grace in order not to hate the guts of some people, however much they deserve it?"

" 'Certainly,' said the engineer heartily, who would have consented to anything" (p. 238). And he goes away, not at all sure what he has heard and seen or what any of it means.

Sutter has directed to Val in his notebooks what is one of the key passages in *The Last Gentleman,* and it concerns Will Barrett's predicament, his "sickness":

Even if you were right. Let us say you were right: that man is a wayfarer (i.e., not transcending being nor immanent being but wayfarer) who therefore stands in the way of hearing a piece of news which is of the utmost importance to him (i.e., his salvation) and which he had better attend to. So you say to him: Look, Barrett, your trouble is due not to a disorder of your organism but to the human condition, that you do well to be afraid and you do well to forget everything which does not pertain to your salvation. . . . What does Barrett do? He attends in that eager flattering way of his and at the end of it he might even say *yes!* But he will receive this news from his high seat of transcendence . . . , throw it into his immanent meat-grinder, and wait to see if he feels better. He told me he's in favor of the World's Great Religions. What are you going to do about that? (p. 276)

But there is one thing about Barrett that Sutter has not seen; indeed, that none of these people has seen. He is that impossible creation of fiction, a good man. Never once in all the course of the book does he act in his own interest—always in the interest of someone else, and always directly, because he cares about or cannot bear to hurt or offend the other person. In him manners are truly morals. All this is done without the faintest hint of the worn-out ostentatious trappings either of "unselfishness" or of sociology that spoil good acts in the days of social Christianity and the welfare state. And pornography—sad or merry—is quite literally impossible to him because he is incapable of using another human being.

In Val Vaught's relationship with her own family and with Will, she is concerned about only one thing; that Jamie receive baptism before he dies; and she attempts to exact a promise both from Will and from Sutter that they will see to this. To Will her obsession with baptism is wholly incomprehensible. He knows nothing of this belief that religion is *the* important thing in a man's life. He was raised an Episcopalian and has never given it a thought. But he is anxious to please, and he is perfectly willing to be the instrument of Jamie's baptism *if* Jamie desires it. But neither he nor Sutter is willing to force on Jamie the direct confrontation with death which the suggestion of baptism will bring about.

The questions of immanence and transcendence which have been raised in the passages above I will return to, but now there are the other members of the Vaught family to consider. Mrs. Vaught never plays a very important role in the book. Poppy, on the other hand, does, and is a true type of man as consumer of goods, man living in the world of immanence. He has a great deal of money, and he is firmly convinced (and with good reason) that money makes the world go round. He is delighted that Will, a young man of impeccable family and an excellent golf player to boot, wants to marry his daughter Kitty; and he would be delighted if Will would take a twenty-thousand-dollar-a-year job in his Chevrolet agency. "I need somebody to help these fellows *close*," he says to Will, gesturing toward the sad salesmen in their Reb-colonel hats wandering the vast floor of his showroom (he owns the second largest Chevrolet agency in the world). "I'd pay twenty thousand a year for just an ordinary good man [who could do that]" (p. 208).

Kitty, in spite of her very lively physical presence, is perhaps the most shadowy character in the book. To Will, she is the very answer to his dreams:

> It was not so much her good looks, her smooth brushed brow and firm round neck bowed so that two or three vertebrae surfaced in the soft flesh, as a certain bemused and dry-eyed expression in which he seemed to recognize—himself! She was a beautiful girl but she also slouched and was watchful and dry-eyed and musing like a thirteen-year-old boy. She was his better half. It would be possible to sit on a bench and eat a peanut-butter sandwich with her and say not a word. (p. 14)

But Kitty, with her Chi O pledge pin, her enthusiasm for the college football team, and her befuddled ideas of how to be a proper fiancée, somehow does not come to life. In order to convince the reader of the reality of Will Barrett's chase after Kitty and of his desire to "wed him a wife and live him a life" *only with her,* Dr. Percy needed to create a woman in whom there resided some concrete quality of being, some basic sanity, that might make Will believe she was the answer to his prayers. And this it seems to me he does not do. I am not convinced that Kitty is notably different from the coed in the early part of the book who gives Barrett the horrors by a few arch remarks addressed to a cat. Of course, Dr. Percy does not mean us to believe that Kitty is "different"; he is actively concerned to prevent our getting any notions about romantic love. But all the same, Barrett could have done a trifle better by himself.

Discussion of the Themes

The philosophical questions which lie behind the story and method of *The Last Gentleman* may be approached in at least two ways. There are first the questions of immanence and transcendence which Sutter attacks so directly in his journals and which are implicitly present in almost every scene in the book. Percy writes most vividly of the nature and horror for a man of living outside the world of being in his account of an event which Will Barrett witnesses in a visit to the Metropolitan Museum of Art:

. . . the air was thick as mustard gas with ravenous particles which were stealing the substance from painting and viewer alike. . . . Here in the roaring twilight the engineer stationed himself and watched people watch the paintings. Sometime ago he had discovered that it is impossible to look at a painting simply so: man-looking-at-a-painting, *voilà!*—no, it is necessary to play a trick such as watching a man who is watching, standing on his shoulders, so to speak. (pp. 28-29)

At any rate, today, it seems to the engineer, it is harder than ever to see anything:

The harder one looked the more invisible the paintings became. Once again the force of gravity increased so that it was all he could do to keep from sinking to all fours.

Yet the young man, who was scientifically minded, held himself sufficiently detached to observe the behavior of other visitors. . . . In they came, smiling, and out they went, their eyes glazed over. The paintings smoked and shriveled in their frames. (p. 29)

Suddenly, without warning, there is a rusty creaking sound and the entire skylight, frame, wheel, chain and all, comes crashing down into the middle of the gallery. Part of it strikes a young workman and knocks him down. "They knelt beside him and bore him up like the mourners of Count Orgaz" (p. 29). The workman is not really hurt; he has just had the breath knocked out of him, but at first no one realizes this:

> As they held him and he gazed up at them, it was as if he were telling them that he could not remember how to breathe. . . .
> It was at this moment that the engineer happened to look under his arm and catch sight of the Velázquez. It was glowing like a jewel. The painter might have just stepped out of his studio and the engineer, passing in the street, had stopped to look through the open door.
> The painting could be seen. (p. 30)

Now, what is Dr. Percy saying in passages like this throughout the book? That the world of being, the physical world in which a man lives as an animal (that is, without self-consciousness), is no longer accessible to him except under the most extraordinary circumstances; that he is alienated from it; that he has shot off into a transcendent orbit from which it is almost if not entirely impossible to re-enter the world of being. A man knows himself to exist and knows his own death as an animal does not. He places himself over against the world and immediately he is no longer a part of it. There have been times and places when a man truly lived in a "place," when his life was a part of the life of the place and partook of its rhythm (this is still true of Uncle Fannin and the Negro Merriam in their absurd life together in Shut Off); and there have been times when a man knew himself as a child of God and transcended the world of being through his love of God. But neither of these things are any longer true for most people in the modern world.

In his article "The Man on the Train," Dr. Percy has written of how other novelists have used the methods of rotation and of repetition to allow their heroes to escape from the suffocating everydayness of their alienation from the world of being. A man suffers amnesia, for example, and it is possible for him to begin an entirely new life with a lovely new wife and lots of delightful new adventures. Or to illustrate the method of repetition, a man goes back, perhaps by accident, to the scenes of his boyhood and there finds the answer to the questions *Who am I? Where did I come from? Where am I going?*

These are methods which a great many novelists have used with more or less success, but which seem to Dr. Percy not to be valid to the handling of the material and the meanings that he is exploring. He writes, "There is no such thing, strictly speaking, as a literature of alienation. In the representing of alienation the category is reversed and becomes something entirely different. There is a great difference between an alienated commuter riding a train and this same commuter reading a book about an alienated commuter riding a train. . . . The reading commuter rejoices in the speakability of his alienation and in the new triple alliance of himself, the alienated character, and the author. His mood is affirmatory and glad. Yes! That is how it is!—which is an aesthetic reversal of alienation."[6]

Here, then, lies the reason why Will Barrett's amnesia never works. He does not stumble into a new and rewarding life. Instead, he wakes up in a greenhouse or on a battlefield haunted by *déjà vus*. He goes back to the scenes of his boyhood, and for a moment it seems that perhaps here, standing outside the house where his aunts still live, touching the iron hitching post that is grown over with the bark of the oak tree, "here in the very curiousness and drollness and extraness of the iron and the bark that—he shook his head—that—The TV studio audience [his aunts are sitting on the gallery watching TV] laughed with its quick, obedient, and above all grateful Los Angeles laughter—once we were lonesome back home, the old sad home of our fathers, and here we are together and happy at last" (p. 260). No, the answer is not here.

Even the romantic quest does not work, the following of the girl of his dreams, but brings only confusion and difficulty and sorrow.

In short, Percy is writing about the alienated man in a way which he hopes will force his reader not to feel cozy in his discovery of another poor fellow who is as alienated as he is and from whom he can learn some answers, but instead to hold the mirror up to his face, and confront his own desolation and despair, and perhaps thereafter begin to look for some new answers.

The second area of philosophical reference in which *The Last Gentleman* may be placed is Kierkegaardian—the three "spheres" of human life: the aesthetic, the ethical, and the religious. The aesthetic and ethical areas we have already considered in the discussion of Will Barrett's family (ethical) and of Rita and Sutter, whose concerns, the first with beauty and experience (ballet dancing and Indian cultism, for example) and the second with beauty and order (the elegance of the scientific method), are both facets of the aesthetic. In his passages about Val, in which the genuineness of her religiosity is questioned but not answered, Dr. Percy has laid the ground work for what he calls a "tentative opening into the religious sphere."

"You see, Barrett," Sutter says, "Val had a dream of what the Church should come to. . . . For example, she did not mind at all if Christendom should be done for, stove in, kaput, screwed up once and for all. She did not mind that the Christers were like everybody else, if not worse. She did not even mind that God shall be gone, absent, not present, A.W.O.L., and that no one noticed or cared, not even the believers. Because she wanted us to go the route . . . and run out of Christendom. . . . There she sits in the woods as if the world had ended and she was one of the Elected Ones Left to keep the Thing going, but the world has not ended, in fact is more the same than usual. We are in the same fix, she and I, only I know it and she doesn't. . . . I do not wait for a sign because there is no sign." (p. 295)

[And then:] "But she changed, you see. . . . *She became hopeful.* . . . She has dealings with the Methodist preacher. . . . She begs from the Seven-Up man and slips him a K.C. pamphlet. . . . She talks the Klonsul into giving her a gym. In short, she sold out. Hell, what she is is a Rotarian." (pp. 295-296)

And, in fact, by the time Will finds Jamie and Sutter in Santa Fe, Sutter has settled upon suicide. He has considered the three choices that he considers available to him: "[to] be a good fellow, healthy and generous, . . . enjoy a beer and a good piece. . . . Or: to live as a Christian among Christians in Alabama? Or to die like an honest man?" (p. 296), and he has decided to die. He is waiting only for Jamie to die and then he intends to shoot himself. Indeed, he has already checked out on the world and on Jamie. He can't even bear to be in the room with Jamie, and has left the care of, and responsibility for, him wholly to the engineer, although it is because of him, Sutter, that Jamie is in New Mexico alone in a strange hospital instead of at home, where he should be, with his mother and his sisters.

And when Will says to him finally, "Then you have nothing to tell me?" Sutter replies that he no longer believes a word of anything he has said or of anything he has written in his casebook. Here, then, is his answer to Will Barrett's question, How shall I live? Die! But Will is too confused and distressed and excited even to hear what Sutter is saying. He knows only that after all there is nothing valuable, no secret that Sutter can impart to him: Sutter did not get his patient to stop screaming by giving him some final, valid answer.

The scene of Jamie's death follows—the most powerful scene in the book. I have read no death in English literature more real or more horrifying. Jamie's death is the sickening dissolution of the body that every man who has watched a death knows and averts his eyes and his soul from. In the midst of the scene, a priest (a bit callous and stupid and bewildered by the irregularity of the request) is administering baptism to Jamie. ("Call a minister," Val has said to Will over the telephone [if you don't want to call a priest] "or do it yourself. I charge you with this responsibility.")

Jamie's answers to the priest are mostly unintelligible, but in two brief passages the author makes it clear that Jamie understands and consents to what is happening.

. . . Jamie's bruised eyes went weaving around to the priest. He said something to the priest which the latter did not understand.
The priest looked up to the engineer.
"He wants to know, ah, why," said the engineer.
"Why what?"
"Why he should believe. . . ."
The priest leaned hard on his fists. "It is true because God Himself revealed it as the truth."
Again the youth's lips moved and again the priest turned to the interpreter.
"He asked how, meaning how does he know that?"
The priest sighed. "If it were not true," he said to Jamie, "then I would not be here. That is why I am here, to tell you."
Jamie, who had looked across to the engineer (Christ, don't look at me!) *pulled down the corners of his mouth in what the engineer perceived unerringly to be a sort of ironic acknowledgment.* [Italics mine.] (p. 314)

And again, at the very end:

Presently the priest straightened and turned to the engineer. . . . "Did you hear him? He said something. What did he say?"

The engineer, who did not know how he knew, was not even sure he had heard Jamie or had tuned him in in some other fashion, cleared his throat.

"He said [and not to his beloved brother, Sutter, nor to his faithful friend, Will, but to this stranger, this chunky, bored priest], 'Don't let me go.'" When the priest looked puzzled, the engineer nodded to the bed and added: "He means his hand, the hand there."

"I won't let you go," the priest said. (p. 316)

Here, and here alone, the author is saying, "Perhaps . . ." and "perhaps" is all he says.

As for Barrett, he has made up his mind, or rather it has come on him like a genuine revelation, so strongly as almost to blow him off his feet, that he must return to his "Bama bride," that there is only one way for him to live, and that that way is to marry, to go to work, and to accept the responsibilities and the contradictions of the world. He has been in the terminal ward, and the possibility that he may begin screaming has been removed. This revelation, which Barrett confesses to Sutter, is put so absurdly, in such trite and stupid words, that it is possible for the reader to believe that Dr. Percy is kidding him, as at first Sutter believes that Will is kidding. But Barrett is not kidding; and one cannot but believe that with him the author is saying: There is no way open to a man to live in this "post-Christian" world except, as Will puts it, "to be a pretty fair member of the community . . . to do something . . . rather than nothing . . . to have a family . . . to love and be loved . . . to make a contribution, however small (pp. 299-300, *passim*). Will even tells Sutter that he and Kitty have agreed by long-distance telephone on a "church home."

I believe it would be a mistake to decide here that Dr. Percy is making fun of Will, that he is deliberately canceling him out. He is simply saying: This is the crazy, phony world we live in, and we, like Will, have to make the best of it.

Sutter, after Jamie's death, gets into his car and starts to drive away into the desert—to his own death. But Will will not let him go. He runs after the car calling to Sutter to stop:

"Dr. Vaught, I need you. . . . I need you more than Jamie needed you. *Jamie had Val, too.*" [Italics mine.]

. . . . as the Edsel took off . . . a final question did occur to [Will] and he took off after it.

"Wait," he shouted in a dead run.

The Edsel paused, sighed, and stopped.

Strength flowed like oil into his muscles and he ran with great joyous ten-foot antelope bounds.

The Edsel waited for him. (pp. 318-319)

Here the book ends, but one is left with the unmistakeable conviction that Sutter has decided that he, too, must wait, must turn back from death, must try to find an answer to that "final question."

NOTE: I have undertaken this discussion of *The Last Gentleman* with considerable assistance in the form of letters from the author. (Whenever material is quoted in this commentary without a source being given, the quotation is from this correspondence.) This is not to say that I set myself up as an authority on what Dr. Percy intends or says, only that he has made some valuable suggestions. As he himself has written, "You could just as easily read *TLG* as a simple story of a young Southern man who goes North and comes home."

I have also benefited from conversations with Shelby Foote and Charles G. Bell regarding various facets of the book and its background.

Notes

1. Ashley Brown, "An Interview with Walker Percy," *Shenandoah*, Spring, 1967, p. 7.
2. *Ibid.*, p. 9.
3. William Alexander Percy, *Lanterns on the Levee* (New York: Knopf, 1941), p. 273.
4. Ashley Brown, *op. cit.*, p. 4.
5. W. A. Percy, *op. cit.*, pp. 312-313.
6. Walker Percy, "The Man on the Train," *Partisan Review*, Fall, 1956, p. 478.